The Kninja Way
Our Journey to Firm of the Future

JULIET AURORA and STEVE LOATES

Copyright © 2018 Juliet Aurora and Steve Loates

All rights reserved.

ISBN: 9781728932880

THE KNINJA WAY

DEDICATION

For all of the entrepreneurs in the world,
who put it all on the line,
each and every day
in search of a dream.

THE KNINJA WAY

CONTENTS

	Acknowledgments	ii
	Foreword	iv
	Introduction	13
	Preface	33
1	WHITE BELT – The New Beginning	37
2	YELLOW BELT – In Our Whitewater	57
3	ORANGE BELT – Calming Seas	85
4	GREEN BELT – Sailing Along	91
5	BLUE BELT – The Shift	125
6	PURPLE BELT – Changing The Focus	139
7	BROWN BELT – Let's Start a New Business	169
8	RED BELT – The Final Chapter – For Now	189
9	BLACK BELT – Enjoy the Ride	215
	Stay in Touch	219

THE KNINJA WAY

ACKNOWLEDGEMENTS

We are so very fortunate to have so many people to thank for being a part of our Journey and for helping us make this book a reality.

Both of our parents who although countries and cultures apart, provided us with the same message – That we could do anything.

Our kids who experienced first hand what growing up in an entrepreneurial family really looks like and through whose eyes we see a better future.

Our grandchildren for their joy and laughter.

Our awesome AIS Kninja team for being the Firm of the Future yesterday, today and tomorrow.

Our fur babies, Sadie, Tiko, Joey, Izzy, and Godfrey for unlimited and unconditional hugs and kisses.

Our coach, Dan for his support and encouragement for making us do the work.

Our Intuit family for providing a helping hand and creating this wave of disruption and excitement in our industry.

Our Tribe and industry colleagues for their unwavering encouragement and willingness to collaborate.

Our editor, Edith, who made the book better and was willing to adapt to our crazy timelines.

For each other. Patience, respect, love and honesty will carry us through anything that comes our way, and set us on the course for our next adventure. Whatever that may be.

And an acknowledgement from Juliet to our daughter, Siera. Thank you for being born. Without you, the business and journey may never have begun.

JULIET AURORA & STEVE LOATES

THE KNINJA WAY

FOREWORD

Have you ever thought of how being in business is a lot like riding a roller coaster for the first time? It can be thrilling and scary and you are never completely sure of what's around the next curve.

And although you can see portions of the roller coaster structure while you wait in line to get on (*thinking about getting into business*), you can't see all of it. Anticipation kicks in as you get securely strapped into your seat (*quit your "real job" and get your business license*). As you slowly climb that first big hill (*set up your accounting, build your website, get your business cards*) and see how high up you are (*sign that line of credit or loan, hire that first employee*), a little fear mixed with excitement begins to build.

Having crested the hill, perched on top and surveyed the track stretching down below you, the excitement can turn into panic (*first sales pitch*). But then it's too late – you are accelerating down the track at breakneck speed, heading towards your first of many loops, hanging on for dear life (*congrats on your first customer*).

Your roller coaster - your business - now has a momentum of its own and you are in motion with it, like it or not!

If you are reading this book you are likely a business

owner and can relate to the roller coaster ride of running a business. You may be looking for advice on how to smooth out the hills and loops, reduce the fear, and increase the excitement – maybe even find the brake lever and have a better sense of control.

Juliet Aurora and Steve Loates have been riding the business owner roller coaster for many years and share their story of how they went from just hanging on, to designing and building their own bigger, faster roller coaster, and loving the ride with hands raised over their heads.

I met Juliet and Steve back in 2011 at a BNI networking group where we were both members. They found out that as a business coach, I help business owners increase their profits, work less, and structure their businesses to work without them. They asked to meet with me to discuss both of their businesses.

When we got together, I learned that they were very unhappy with how business was going. They had been in business for several years, and were working extremely long hours. Their profitability was suffering, and their team was not ideal. They saw very little of each other or their family. Steve and Juliet were frustrated, tired and stressed. But at the same time, they were committed to making their business a success, and committed to doing the learning and self-development required to be successful.

We began working together and they consistently applied and educated themselves, learned from their mistakes, forged new paths, learned to say "no," committed to their future, committed to taking action, and never gave up. Seven years later, they own a fantastic bookkeeping business and have been recognized and admired globally as an innovative example of success in the bookkeeping world.

Steve and Juliet learned a lot along the way, and I know you will get a lot out of their story, and take away some of the lessons that they learned the hard way.

It is said that experience is a tough teacher as she gives the test first, and the lesson second. Juliet and Steve are sharing their experience, so you can get the lessons *before* the tests!

Through their story, you'll learn:

When to say "no" and put yourself first. Many entrepreneurs put their clients first which is a recipe for burnout and resentment.

How and when to fire a client. You likely have some clients in need of firing right now – for their own good, and your sanity.

How to push through fear. Things can seem scary until you take some action as Juliet will show you.

The power of using simple systems. Learn how to use systems to free yourself from busy-work, and focus on achieving your goals.

Getting out of your own way. You have a team, or subcontractors for a reason – to make your life easier, not the other way around!

How to create a business – not just a job. A business runs without you – in a job, the business runs you!

How to persist in the face of challenges. Lessons on not giving up!

And many more insightful lessons on how to master your business roller coaster.

It makes me super proud to see the kind of abundance-minded, balanced, successful, respected business owners that Steve and Juliet have become, and I am honoured to have played a small part in their journey.

I know they will be honoured to have played a small role in your success by sharing their story with you. Enjoy the ride!

Dan Holstein

CEO, Kaizen Performance Improvement Corporation

THE KNINJA WAY

INTRODUCTION

Our goal with this book is to share OUR entrepreneurial story so that it helps YOU with YOUR journey. Help you avoid the mistakes that we made. Help you get to where you want to go faster and with less stress. Please don't believe for a second that just because you read our journey that you will not make any mistakes. Because you will. But they will be your mistakes, and will end up being a part of YOUR story.

The role of an entrepreneur is much like riding on a roller coaster. It is often filled with lots of sleepless nights as well as many exciting days. But more than anything else, being an entrepreneur puts YOU in charge of your own destiny, and what more can you possibly ask for?

Over the years we have seen many quotes about entrepreneurship but this one is probably our favourite.

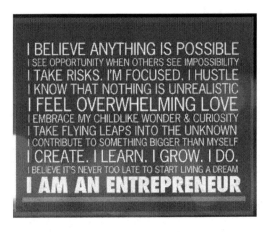

We both come from completely different backgrounds, and different viewpoints, so we've tried to lay this book out a little differently than others you may see on the bookshelves. Much of this book is written in the first tense - primarily Juliet's voice (which is pretty typical - but as you'll see, Steve is never silent about expressing his opinion.) You may resonate more with one or the other of us, but we hope that you will learn from both.

So let's get this party started.

Steve and Juliet

Juliet's Story

My name is Juliet Aurora. And I am an entrepreneur.

If someone had told me when I started my business in the year 2000, that 18 years later I would be writing a book about my journey, I would have told them that they were crazy. Even if they told me that it was a certainty, I would have told them that they were crazy! Never, in the remote recesses of my mind when I took the plunge into self-employment all of those years ago, would writing a book about being in business have crossed my mind. At the time, it was fear, and sleepless nights, and "what if this doesn't work" conversations. The journey certainly wasn't an uphill trajectory all the way. There were a lot of peaks and valleys and some years more valleys than peaks. So I guess that is why I wanted to write this book with Steve. To give hope. To tell those out there, who are questioning whether to take that leap of faith, or hang up that sign, that there is hope. That anything is possible.

So here goes…. <u>AIS Solutions</u> started out as Aurora International Services (AIS) in the spare bedroom of my semi-detached house in Toronto, Ontario, Canada in the year 2000. The name arose because I thought it made me sound bigger, and at the time, if your name was included in your business name, you didn't have to spend the $60 to formally register the name, so I was also being cheap. (That's frugal in business owner speak!)

I had no grand aspirations of a business at the time. I just didn't like how much time my daughter was spending in daycare, and I honestly felt like I was missing out on so much. I had a corporate job and so I started AIS really small. I dipped my toe in the water to see what happened, but did not really commit to anything or really put anything on the line. Fast forward just over one year, when fate intervened and sent some signals my way. I went through a messy divorce and became a single mom. The company I was working for at the time was purchased by an international conglomerate and being relocated to the US. It was still too close to 9/11 and the colour of my skin was not conducive to living in the US. So it was do or die. Either I throw myself into this venture and give myself the freedom to spend time with my daughter, or I pound the pavement and find another job. Don't ask me why I chose the former. I certainly didn't think of myself as an entrepreneur. I didn't view myself as a leader of any sort, or a visionary. I simply was trying to have a little control of my life and my time and be able to play with my daughter and read her stories whenever she wanted. I gave myself six months. That was about what I had in funds that I could survive on if I didn't have a single client or make a dime. If after the six months I couldn't support myself and my daughter, I told myself that I would go back into the corporate world.

That was 2002.

My first client ended up being my former employer. My second client was in Barbados, as a spin-off from my first client. My third client was my real estate agent. My fourth client was her friend. And then it just morphed from there. My clients grew from word of mouth, and I pretty much performed any service that was related to finance: taxes, accounting department support, year-end assistance, bookkeeping, accounting, and accounting system conversions. If there was a job that was related to numbers in any way, shape or form, I took it. I worked in the morning before my daughter woke up, played with her in the mornings, dropped her off for a couple of hours at daycare, and then worked again after she went to bed. There were long days and nights, but I was energized. I had control of my life and had clients who allowed me to pay my bills, keep a roof over my head, and put food on the table.

My business ran as just me until about 2006, when I hired my first subcontractor. By then, I had met Steve and relocated my business to Burlington, Ontario, so that he and I could be together. That story is probably a book all on its own, as there was a great deal of discussion as to whether I was moving to Burlington or he was moving to Toronto. He won.

From 2006 to 2010, the business ran from my home in Burlington with staff meetings around my dining table. As I found that there was too much disparity in what was passing as bookkeeping for small business, I started offering Bookkeeping and CFO Services as a package. My subcontractors provided the bookkeeping and I contributed the CFO skill-set.

My business continued this way for many years with me working all the time. Having an office in my home. Getting up in the morning and heading to the office. Going to the office before going to bed at night. Work/life balance was a myth. It didn't exist, and there was no separation for me. I didn't have the personality or the discipline to ever turn it off.

In 2010, I took what I believe was my first big leap into the business world by moving the business out of my home. It was also the birth of AIS Solutions. Aurora International Services disappeared, and we created this exciting new business. Steve had always been my silent partner with Aurora International Services. He was my sounding board, my voice of reason, my biggest ally and support system, all while still running his own retail business at the time. But in 2010, we formalized that participation and he joined AIS Solutions part-time to help build this conglomerate that would shake up the bookkeeping world. Or at least that was our goal.

Most of this book will be about the journey from 2010 to present day, as that is when I started really treating it like a business.

The last eight years have been unbelievable for us. I'm not going to tell you that it has all run smoothly from 2010 to now because I would be lying - remember the roller-coaster analogy. There were days that we seriously thought about closing the doors, and that perhaps it wasn't all worth putting everything on the line.

At the end of 2015, Steve joined AIS Solutions full time, and we entered into another exciting phase of our business journey – the creation of Kninja. Kninja is our way of giving back ... giving back to this bookkeeping industry of mostly solo home-based businesses that have the same struggles that I did. It is our way of sharing all of the mistakes that we've made so that perhaps others can accelerate their path and not have the same low valleys that we did over the years.

That really is the reason that Steve and I decided to write this book. Actually Steve decided about a year and a half ago, and it took him that long to convince me that we should.

We will share with you all that it isn't easy. It is scary. It is a bumpy road. There are days and months and years, when you just want to slam the doors shut and hide in a corner. But hang in. There is light at the end of the tunnel. It is all possible. Don't give up, because quite honestly, it is worth the ride.

Steve's Story

My name is Steve Loates and I am an entrepreneur.

My journey began many years before Juliet's, way back in 1983. Yes, I am that old...although I much prefer the word experienced.

I learned very early on in my business career that my best path was probably going to be working for myself. Within the first three years of graduating college with a degree in electronics, I found myself starting and ending five different jobs with five different companies. With the first couple of jobs I was convinced that I had just not found the right situation for me. But, after jobs four and five, even *I* had to admit the problem was not the five companies. I hated to admit it, but I appeared to be the common thread. It became very apparent that I had a problem with authority, following instructions I didn't believe in and having others tell me what to do. My mom called it an independent streak; I called it strong willed and my dad had a completely different name for it.

I was an only child and so I believe from an early age that greatly influenced my independent streak. Without siblings to argue with, I always got my own way and making decisions and setting my own direction became second nature to me.

I have also always been a bit of an overachiever. At the age of 24 I became the youngest Regional Sales Manager in the history of the wholesale company I was working for, producing triple digit growth in just over 18 months. That was followed by the job offer that would start me on my entrepreneurial path. At 27, one of my retail accounts was looking to expand and needed a manager to look after their newest retail location. At this point I had zero experience in retail, but having observed my own retail clients I believe I knew why some were successful and some were not.

However, I was hesitant at accepting the new role. Although the offer was very appealing, the truth was I didn't need it. I already had a good job, nice salary with bonuses, car, expense account, travel. But, they were persistent and finally they asked that all important question...what would it take? I had always believed the best time to negotiate is when you really don't care about the outcome and so I said. "I am interested, but am not willing to give up this job for another job...if you want me it must include the opportunity for ownership - I want to be master of my own ship...I want a piece of the next business I am going to help build. We went back and forth and concluded an agreement that was fair to everyone. I would have complete autonomy to run the business and if it reached certain goals I would be given the opportunity to buy 33% of the business. It was during my retail journey that I also learned that full autonomy *also* meant full responsibility for success and failure. And so, it began.

Up until then I had never experienced much self-doubt, but it hit me then when I thought about what I had done...given up a great salary and benefits for the opportunity to run a brand new retail business with zero experience. What did I know about retail? I had never worked a day in a retail store. Had I completely lost my mind?

Things began well. We had a great first year - very profitable. The second year was even better as I reached the necessary goals and in 1985 I became a co-owner in the business. The problem was that the early success had made me blind to the things I didn't know about retail and in year four reality set in. Our top line was over $2.0 million and our bottom line was a minus $19,000. My partners were not impressed (remember, I had autonomy) and I was angry and frustrated. How could we possibly be losing money?

This brought me to the second important step in my entrepreneurial journey. I decided I needed to understand what was going on financially and learn what I didn't know. So, I called my accountant and told him that I wanted to understand every number, every line and every note on our financial statements. Fortunately, he was the type of accountant who wanted to help. He was patient and gave me a crash course in financial statements and taught me why I shouldn't only look at my Income statement.

Fast forward as I bought my partners out and grew my retail business from one location to two to three to four and then back to one. I should explain at this point that I don't believe in success and failure...only success and learnings. And, I can tell you there was lots of both during those years.

I became fascinated with computers and technology,

but most of all with the web and the opportunities it presented for small businesses like mine. This was 1997, long before Social Media, Email Marketing or even Google. For a number of reasons, I knew that in order for my business to continue and prosper we needed a website so we could take advantage of this thing called the World Wide Web. And, so over the next year or so I learned how to build websites and created one for my own business. The next page is a screenshot of my masterpiece from October 1998. There was no such thing as mobile versions at that time, so definitely not responsive to screen size. Images, videos or flash was definitely not the norm as the speed of the internet connection was dial up (remember that!). It was pretty much just a page of text with some colour.

THE KNINJA WAY

STEVE LOATES KEYBOARD CENTRE

WELCOMES YOU!

Last Updated October 27, 1996

We have been serving the southern Ontario region of Canada since 1983. We offer top quality Yamaha Musical Instruments at competitive prices supported by a complete range of customer services. We are located in the Golden Horseshoe region of Ontario with stores in Burlington and Hamilton. Each location offers a complete selection of name brand New and Used Pianos (Digitals, Uprights and Grands), Keyboards, Guitars, Printed Music and Computer Music Software.

We have sold over 650,000 keys!

* Lowest Price Guarantee * 30 Day Price Protection on all purchases

Keyboard Centre News!

YAMAHA ACOUSTIC PIANOS (Grands and Uprights) - Yamaha Pianos are the "First Choice" of the Royal Conservatory of Music in Toronto and are the choice of more teachers, churches, recording studios, artists and universities than any other piano in the world today. Both of our locations also carry a good selection of refurbished used pianos, both uprights and grands. All of our used pianos carry a full warranty, a trade-in guarantee and our exclusive buy back guarantee.

YAMAHA HYBRID PIANOS (Disklavier, MIDI Series and GranTouch) - The *Disklavier* is available in an upright or Grand model. It is essentially a **piano** in it. A world class acoustic piano, a reproducing piano utilizing computer technology, a recording piano and a MIDI piano. It is the ultimate home entertainment centre.

The *MIDI Piano* is a new type of acoustic piano with MIDI capability. It features a quick shift system which can stop the hammers from hitting the strings effectively silencing the piano to all outside ears. Sophisticated electronics then take over reproducing the same rich tones through stereo earphones. *GranTouch* incorporates the latest digital technology to produce the most realistic piano sound while keeping the touch and feel of an acoustic piano through the use of a true piano action.

YAMAHA CLAVINOVA DIGITAL PIANOS - Leading edge technology and innovations have made the Yamaha Clavinova the best selling digital piano in the world today. Due to the outstanding sound and real piano touch the *Clavinova* is the "First Choice" of the largest music school in Canada, the Royal Conservatory of Music in Toronto. There are 12 models available providing an instrument to suit every budget and lifestyle.

YAMAHA ELECTRONIC KEYBOARDS - We carry a complete line of portable electronic Keyboards from the very basic to professional models with Touch Sensitive Keys, Floppy Disk Drive and MIDI compatibility. Whatever your budget or musical taste we have something for you!

GUITARS - We offer YAMAHA, MONTANA & APPLAUSE by OVATION acoustic classical and steel string guitars including 12-string models and the very popular acoustic-electric models. We also have a complete selection of related accessories, including cases, tuners, strings, straps, stands and instructional videos.

RENTED MUSIC SHEETS and BOOKS for pianos and guitar (popular titles and methods). We stock one of the largest selections of printed sheet music and books in the region. From popular movies and show tunes, Disney, classics, jazz, big band, alternative, new age and rock n roll. We have it all! Our computerized stock ordering and mail ordering systems allow us to order items and mail them to you within a few days.

COMPUTER MUSIC SOFTWARE - We have software available for your PC or Mac. You can create your own digital recording studio, write and print your own musical score, learn how to play or just have fun. We also stock MIDI interface cards, adaptors and cables.

Printed Music and Computer Music Software are available by mail order.
Mastercard & Visa Welcome – Same Day Shipping

MUSIC LESSONS: We offer private instruction for all ages and levels in Piano, Keyboard, Guitar, Theory and Voice. Our teachers are dedicated professionals who were chosen based upon their musical and communication skills, but most importantly their ability to motivate students. Ask about our money back summer!

Rudimentary yes, but also effective. I can still remember my excitement the first time the telephone rang in our showroom from someone who had visited our website. The world had become a much smaller place. Later still I was able to add a successful e-commerce business to my bricks and mortar store, which we grew and later sold. Throughout this time I became an avid student of online marketing and how it could help our business to grow - social media, online advertising, email marketing, SEO - I immersed myself into all of it.

By now, Juliet and I had met and were partners in life and business, helping each other to grow both of our firms.

I love building businesses and since I had a great manager running my retail business, it helped me to start another business that focused on helping other small businesses with their online marketing and websites. As the online marketing and web company grew, it didn't take long before I decided to close the retail business and focus my energy on building the online marketing business as well as continuing to help Juliet with AIS Solutions.

And this leads us to 2015. I had now closed the retail business, sold the e-commerce business and was continuing with the online marketing. However, I wasn't happy. I don't think my heart was ever fully committed to the online marketing business. I could see the potential in AIS Solutions and I truly believed if both Juliet and I were focused on only one business - AIS Solutions - that we could build it into something special.

So, we wound down the online marketing and consulting firm and I joined AIS Solutions on an official full-time basis where I would be responsible for the Business Development so Juliet could focus her talents and energy on Operations, Team Building and Training.

It is all of the above experiences that gave me a completely different perspective, and more importantly, brought different skill sets, to AIS Solutions as we embarked on this journey together.

STEVE

Our Story

You've heard each of our individual stories, but this book is really **Our** Story. We are often asked how we met, and how we can possibly manage working together and still remain married.

So how we met. It's actually not some grand romantic story to share. We met at a Financial Forum conference. Yup. Not exciting or glamorous at all. Aren't you glad you asked? We ended up sitting next to each other, chatting during breaks and meals, and the rest is history. (There's actually a longer story, but we will leave that for our second book.)

As we both mentioned in our individual stories, there was a lot of advice crossing over in both directions as we ran independent businesses. But we also ultimately understood that the Retail and then the e-Commerce business were Steve's and AIS was Juliet's. So that also meant that the final decision was up to one individual, no matter what.

When Steve joined AIS full time, that was probably one of the biggest concerns we had. It consumed our discussions because we are both fairly strong personalities, and we would never want to find that our marriage had suffered because we were in business together. That just wasn't an option.

Our solution was to divide the business functions by responsibility. One domain would be Juliet's. The other would be Steve's. Major decisions would be discussed, but the ultimate decision if it involved Business Development, Sales or Marketing would be Steve's. If the decision to be made involved Operations, Team or Training, then the decision would be Juliet's. No hard feelings, no disputes, no conflict.

We've been operating that way since we started and about 99% of the time it works. And works well. It allows us to apply our individual strengths, but utilize the strength and differing viewpoint of the other. It truly is one of the reasons we believe that we've thrived as both business partners and life partners.

THE KNINJA WAY

Preface

No matter which business expert you follow, they all say pretty much the same thing, just using different terminology. However, the message is exactly the same. Every business, regardless of industry, goes through a predictable series of steps from the day it starts. If you were to look at successful businesses, failed businesses, it doesn't matter. The successful ones have evolved through the various stages. The failed ones died off in one of the stages. And some businesses get stuck in a particular stage.

ActionCoach calls it the six phases of business. Les McKeown calls it his stages of Predictable Success. Some experts have five stages, some have six, some have four. They all vary a little, but fundamentally they are all the same.

The moment you open your doors as a business, you are in the business lifecycle. It's not a choice that you make. You can't opt out. It's just a fact. You have started the business lifecycle. How you progress through those stages, or if you EVEN progress through them; that's up to you.

As you've probably learned so far about Steve and me, we aren't people who like the status quo. We tend to think about how we could improve things, so of course, we've created our own version of the stages of a business.

1 - White Belt
2 - Yellow Belt
3 - Orange Belt
4 - Green Belt
5 - Blue Belt
6 - Purple Belt
7 - Brown Belt
8 - Red Belt
9 - Black Belt

As you progress through the chapters, we will provide you with our definitions of the belts.

One common fallacy that needs to be clarified is the "black belt as master" stereotype. In reality, a black belt indicates the wearer is competent in basic technique and is now ready for more advanced learning.

Let's dive in.

THE KNINJA WAY

1 WHITE BELT
– THE NEW BEGINNING (2010)

White Belt: A white belt is a novice beginning their search for knowledge.

"Being in business should give you more life....not less." - Brad Sugars, CEO of ActionCoach

As we mentioned in our opening chapters, the majority of this book is going to be about what happened to us, what we did, and our mistakes and successes from 2010 onwards as that is when we really started to treat AIS Solutions as a business. Prior to 2010, it was just a great way for me to have a job and work from home. There were no real aspirations to grow Aurora International Services to anything of substance. Yes, I wanted my top line revenue number to grow. I wanted to make more money, but that was pretty much it. There was no planning, no strategy, I pretty much just winged it.

So let me tell you about 2010. I incorporated AIS Solutions in March of 2010 and Steve became a full and legal partner of my business. One simple sentence there, but so much angst and worry and sleepless nights. I felt like I was finally putting on my big girl pants and stepping into the big leagues.

So why all the fear?

#1 - I've got overhead, so had better make some money.

Before now, if I had a tough month, or if my A/R was behind, it wasn't that big of a deal. I could make do and stretch out some stuff. Steve also was still running his own business full time, so we had a good solid income that my business, or lack thereof, would never cause us to be on the street. As soon as I put my name on that lease agreement though, that changed. I now had rent that I had to pay EVERY month regardless of what money flowed into my bank account.

#2 - I've got to be at the office every day.

One of the things I loved about being in business for myself was that I was the boss. So if I didn't want to work today, no one was going to tell me that I had to be there. I was a horrible employee when I was working for others. But working for myself, I was pretty darn good. But now, it felt different. It felt like I needed to be at the office every day, from 8:00 a.m. to 4:00 p.m. or 9:00 to 5:00. But every day. And all day.

#3 - I've got to hire people.

Actually that's not true. I didn't HAVE to hire people. I could have just left it as being me, but considering that I had just rented office space with two offices, a boardroom and an open area for four desks, it seemed quite silly to not hire people. I might as well have just stayed at home. But along with the fear of hiring people and having to always pay them a salary, it was also knowing that whether AIS Solutions succeeded or failed, there were now other families that would be affected. And the responsibility of that terrified me.

"I learned that courage was not the absence of fear, but the triumph over it. The brave man is not he who does not feel afraid, but he who conquers that fear." - Nelson Mandela

I probably need to backtrack here and maybe explain why we decided to make this big leap in 2010 and not just continue on my merry way of running the business from my house.

My business model as Aurora International Services was this:

- All work was done onsite at the client's office
- All work was billed hourly
- All work was billed after the work was completed
- I had subcontractors who completed the bookkeeping, and I did the CFO work
- I worked a lot. I worked in the mornings before I went to clients.
- I worked a lot. I worked in the evenings, after dinner and returning from clients.
- I worked a lot. I worked weekends, when I thought how awesome it was that I didn't have to be at a client's.

One of the subcontractors that I had hired under Aurora International Services was a gentleman named Neville. I had an existing client who was taking over operations of a new business and wanted me to do the Controllership oversight and bring in a team with me to do the day-to-day bookkeeping and turn their existing accounting department around. I didn't have an existing team member who could commit five days a week to one company, and they were located about 45 minutes away from my home office in Burlington.

So I decided to interview and hire someone brand new, more local to this new business, for this new role. Enter Neville. Neville's resume popped into my inbox eight minutes after I posted the job online. He was extremely overqualified for this position, which I told him in my initial response to him. But he was convincing, had all of the right answers to my initial questions so I met with him. He had only recently moved to Canada. He had no Canadian experience, but had a wealth of knowledge in accounting and finance from his previous job - the CFO of a multi-billion company (yes, that was not a typo). He also had a law degree and a finance degree. But he couldn't get a job in Canada because he had no Canadian experience. I know, crazy! Long story short, (although it may be too late for that already), I hired Neville to be one of my bookkeepers at the previously mentioned client for a year-long contract.

He was so over qualified and such an amazing big thinker, that when we started AIS Solutions, he was my first hire as an employee. The work at the client I had hired him for had wound up, so I really had no work for him to do under this new AIS Solutions umbrella, but I knew that he was going to be important for the strategy of my business.

So where was I? Right, I was talking about why we decided to make the big leap in 2010. And quite honestly, one of the reasons was Neville. I felt that between the knowledge of Steve, myself and now Neville, we could do some amazing things and create a kick ass company. I didn't want to waste that talent and knowledge by placing him as a bookkeeper somewhere else.

The other reason was that I was working too much. My personality didn't seem to have the discipline to not walk into the office in my house and not work. So a big part of moving into a separate office was Steve's insistence as he was watching me burn out, even though I also knew that something needed to change. The unspoken rule became that if I wasn't in the AIS office, I shouldn't be working.

But to be honest, I had enough fears about that first big move that I could write an entire book about that.

#4 - My relationship with Steve.

As I told you at the beginning, I went through a divorce. That is an ugly thing to happen to anyone, and probably more so if you are in the Indian culture, where it was the worst thing that could ever happen to a female (yet another book!). Steve and I had been together for a little while by then, and we had a good thing going. We were happy, and, were true partners in life. I've heard the horror stories of being in business with your husband, and I was worried that going into business with Steve was going to mess up the great thing we had.

#5 - Fear of Failure.

What if it didn't work? I come from a pretty high

expectation family, with a high achiever older sister whose footsteps I rarely felt like I could live up to.

What if this whole thing didn't work?

> **STEVE'S SLANT**
>
> As I am sure you can imagine, we had many discussions before making this move and some were very emotional. We were both worried about what this might do to our relationship. I already had my own established business and now we were looking to open another one with its own demands.
>
> We had heard all the advice and feedback about the dangers of spouses working together in the same business and here we were jumping right in.
>
> Was this the right decision for both of us? Why were we doing this? Would it bring us closer together or drive us apart? How long could our relationship bear this strain?
>
> We were both coming off divorces and had gotten together as a couple because we wanted to be with each other.
>
> Despite all of these fears something inside both of us said we had to do this.
>
> I can remember reading somewhere that there are two types of people in the world - those who like to ride on roundabouts and those who prefer the rollercoaster.
>
> It was pretty obvious that we were about to jump on that roller coaster together. Hopefully, we would enjoy the ride.

The title of this chapter was The New Beginning,

which sounded beautiful as we were coming up with the outline for the book. But after writing these pages, all I remember was the noise in my head. It certainly wasn't a quiet beginning.

The quiet was probably from the lack of the phone ringing, or clients at our door. Because not only did we have to address all of the fears that I've mentioned above, we also decided to fundamentally change my business model from what I had been doing for the first 10 years of my business. Not just a few small changes, but fundamentally shift everything.

Here is what the business model of AIS Solutions looked like when we opened the doors:

I'll put it side by side with what the business looked like before, so you can see the difference without having to flip back through the pages.

Aurora International Services	AIS Solutions
All work was done onsite at the client's office	All work done at AIS offices. No onsite work at clients Remote services only. We provided the hosting, backup and firewalls.
All work was billed hourly	Fixed monthly rate services
All work was billed after the work was completed	All billing was at the 1st day of the month, before any work was completed
I had subcontractors who completed the bookkeeping, and I did the CFO work	I have employees who complete the work, and I did the CFO work.

Remember Fear #5? *Fear of Failure.*

"Face your fear so you can live your dreams." - Les Brown

Our Business Model

So why did we change our business model? More than anything we wanted to be different than anything else that was in our industry. So we objectively sat back and looked at the bookkeeping function from Steve's small business experience, and said: "From the business owner perspective, what would I want from my accounting professional?" One of the biggest things that emerged was having no idea what the bill was going to be every month. As a business owner, he was budgeting for everything else, but his bookkeeping bill was always a surprise. Sometimes good, sometimes bad, but always a surprise - so **Fixed Fees** were born.

The second biggest challenge was the space and keeping up with the software and updates. He didn't have an administration person at his store, and in retail, maximizing selling space was key, so his office was tiny. Whenever the bookkeeper came in, she would be in a small space in the corner of his office - so **No Onsite** was born.

And the last one was timing. Because he didn't need a full time bookkeeper, she would come in one or two days a week which meant that he was always at least a week behind in his numbers. And if he unexpectedly needed a cheque during the week, or got a call from a supplier, he either had to deal with it himself, or the person had to wait until his bookkeeper was in next.

This was the toughest to address, but we addressed it with **virtually hosted books** - we could work for an hour a day on the client if they needed, or could address unexpected requests throughout the week. We called this service *AIS Cloud* (I guess we were ahead of our time!)

Needless to say, 2010 was a time of my life that I was so excited and so scared, all at the same time. Some days the emotions would see-saw back and forth within the hour. I had a pretty good thing going up until then. In my best year working solo with subcontractors, I was earning almost $300K per year.

So why was I putting all that at risk? Not necessarily because I thought that I'd make more money. I was going all in because what I was doing wasn't sustainable. It all relied on me and the endless hours that I was putting in each and every day, seven days a week. The very reason that I had entered into business for myself - time with my daughter - had gotten lost somewhere. Sure, I was making money from the subcontractors I had working for me, but the big dollars were coming from my sweat and sleepless nights.

And did I mention that I came from a family with high expectations? Between being told that I was set out for greatness from my childhood, to Steve's love of building businesses, it was just a natural progression -

to see what could be built.

So March 2010, we moved into our first official office space. The team at the office consisted of myself, Steve, Neville and Jessica - an office administrator/marketing/part-time law student who we had hired to help us get this off the ground.

(A little side note and funny story - one of the things that our new hires always had to do on their first day of starting with us was assemble their own chair, as we pretty much bought things as we needed them.)

We had Steve and me sharing an office, Neville in the office beside us, a boardroom, and Jessica in the open area with desks ready for our next three people.

Here's the picture that we hung on the wall between mine and Steve's desks.

What we loved about this picture was the line that represented the two of us perfectly. "Every great oak tree started out as a couple of nuts who stood their ground". Yup. Us completely.

At this point, quite honestly, it seemed like all we were doing was spending money.

- Rebranding - with a new logo, from Aurora International Services to AIS Solutions
- Building a new website with our new services and new name
- Big digital white screen in the boardroom to wow all of our potential new clients
- Office furniture for seven
- Servers, terminal servers, VPN's, firewall boxes - as we were now hosting all of our client's data

It was just cheque after cheque after cheque, pulling out that credit card, over, and over and over again. (Although we certainly did earn a lot of points on those credit cards during those months.)

First Client

Neville's primary role was to find us some staff. None of my subcontractors wanted full time work, so they were continuing with the Aurora International existing client base, doing onsite work and maintaining the status quo for the time being. I was still doing onsite CFO work, but not taking on any new projects. I was in search of clients. New clients.

Cloud wasn't a word back then - I believe we were still calling it "the web." A cloud didn't represent anything more than fluffy white gas in the sky, let alone being a part of the regular vernacular of a small business owner's language. So my sales pitch to potential new clients was long and lengthy, mostly educational and certainly not smooth.

Every one of my clients for Aurora International had come to me organically - by referral, or word of mouth. No one had come to me because of my bare bones website - it was pretty much just something pretty that I could look at - and I had never spent a single dollar on active marketing or advertising.

That all changed with the opening of AIS Solutions and overhead costs needing to be covered. So far, Neville's salary, Jessica's salary, and all those numerous cheques I mentioned above were coming from our savings.

Then we got our first client 22 days after we opened our doors. They found us via our new website (Yay!) and liked our sales pitch and USP's of being all remote, duplicate staff support, fixed fee, and supervised by accountants. Little did they know that when we signed them on, we didn't have one bookkeeper on staff, forget about two for duplicate staff support. But I obviously was convincing enough in the story I told about our business and what we could offer.

"Marketing is no longer about the stuff you make or sell, but about the stories you tell." - Seth Godin

---

Neville's search for an employee went into overdrive and we hired our first staff member. Neville had been the front facing person with this new client until then, and he also had been doing most of the work, as we tried to get this new employee up and running quickly. But we made the first mistake that most small business owners do, and hired from a place of panic and desperation, not a good combination to find the best talent. I think that our new hire was with us for about two weeks before we let him go and moved on to our second hire. Our client had never met Employee #1, so when we eventually transitioned the client from Neville to this new employee, he had no idea of the upheaval that had been happening behind the scenes at our end.

And so our business continued on for the next eight months. We would get a handful of new clients - Steve taking time out from his own business to come in on some of the bigger sales calls since he had a much better sales process than I did. Then Neville would go in search of new staff. Hopefully they would work out. Some did. Some didn't. Our shortest lived staff member started with us on a Monday morning at 8:30 a.m., had training in the morning, left for lunch and never came back. Then took us to the Employment Board to ensure she got paid for those four hours. I know ...the stories we could tell!

Our First Awesome Team Member

Jessica decided to go back to school full time during that time period and so Neville went off again in search of a new person. Can you read between the lines and see how much of Neville's time was spent on hiring staff? This was not a good use of all of those strategic and planning skills we wanted to capitalize on initially.

Jessica was replaced by Amy who remained with us for seven years until she decided to have some babies. But we learned something fundamental with the hire of Amy. She came from a childhood of growing up with small business owner parents. She got it. She knew that her job title and description was irrelevant. She understood that in a business our size, it was a constantly moving target, and she would jump in for whatever needed to be done. There were days that Amy was the only person in our office, so she definitely jumped in everywhere. She was an awesome team member - probably our first great team member - and we know she will be an even more awesome mom!

We were at two full time bookkeepers by the end of 2010, with Neville overseeing the team, me overseeing the work, providing CFO services, and making sales calls, while Steve was ramping up our marketing.

That's the way that we grew for the first year. One client at a time, one staff member at a time. At the end of year one being AIS Solutions, we had five full time staff. It's a pretty typical path I think. Slow and steady. Nothing earth shattering. Nothing mind blowing. Nowhere near as steep of a growth curve as we had envisioned. Most of our time seemed to be spent on being reactionary, putting out fires as they arose, and not having a clear, defined path of what direction we were going, other than one foot in front of the other.

> **STEVE'S SLANT**
> When I look back on that first year I cannot believe how much happened at AIS Solutions. Not too many successes, but lots and lots of learning. We knew it was going to get better, if for no other reason than Juliet and I would accept nothing less. Little did we know how many learnings we still had coming our way.

"The journey of a thousand miles begins with a single step." - Lao Tzu

LESSONS LEARNED:

1. We always have a choice when it comes to FEAR. Forget Everything And Run or, the one we decided upon Face Everything And Rise.
2. Don't accept the status quo. Always be willing to take a chance and evolve into something better.

2 YELLOW BELT
- IN OUR WHITEWATER (2011)

Yellow Belt: A yellow belt has started with baby steps seeing their first ray of knowledge.

Here's where the real challenges began. Neither Steve nor I had yet taken a dime in salary or dividend, or anything from the business at this point. The money was all flowing one way. From our bank account to AIS. We would certainly have odd months where we didn't have to put anything into the business, but we also were not taking anything out.

But worse than all of that - I wasn't working any less. The plan of me only working when I was at the AIS offices was so far from reality. If anything, I was working more, because of all of the fear that this wouldn't succeed and how much of our savings we had poured into it. It was also now going on two years since Steve and I had taken a vacation which meant the pressure in our personal lives was also building.

We tried escaping for a week to the sun, but spent most of the vacation connected to our team, and our clients, or working, that I'm not sure we didn't come back feeling more burned out than before we had left, and also having spent more money out of our savings.

However, the one thing that has been consistent with Steve and me, no matter what is going on around us, is that we make some of our best decisions when we are on the beach. (You'll see this as a theme throughout the last 10 years). When we went on this vacation we realized that something had to give.

Taking A Step Back

In early 2011, with sadness and regret we sat down with Neville and told him that we could no longer afford to keep him. It was one of the toughest conversations that I've ever had in business, and I could probably recite it for you verbatim. We thought that what we needed was not strategy and planning but someone who could take things off of my plate and alleviate some of my workload. We weren't prepared to hire another person and fund it personally, so we parted ways with Neville and went in search of an Account Manager. We needed someone who had enough experience to provide oversight to my bookkeepers, and take over some of the bookkeeping that kept landing on my plate. Exit Neville from AIS Solutions, but not from our lives. We still keep in touch with Neville to this day.

> **STEVE'S SLANT**
> As a business owner I have found that the thing I hate the most is letting people go. If you care about people at all you will never get used to it...you will never want to get used to it. But, this particular case with Neville was especially difficult as it felt like a big step back for everyone.
> Obviously, we were putting Neville in a very unpleasant situation, but I really felt he was someone who could help us get to where we needed to go. However, at this point we were also much more in survival mode than thinking about how we could get to the next level.

In April 2011, I thought that we had found that person. I must tell you, that I was so excited when we hired her. I envisioned all of this free time in my future. I spent every waking moment at the office training her, and grooming her, and transferring all of the knowledge that was in my head so that she could take all of this stuff off my plate. What I was going to do with this free time, I had no idea, maybe actually have AIS Solutions take over the world, like we had originally planned.

Sadly, I have to report that it didn't happen. Instead, we ended up in greater state of chaos than we were previously. Now there were two of us working days and nights and weekends. Things were falling through the cracks. As aggressively as we were bringing on new clients into the top of the funnel, they were dropping out the bottom and we ended up in exactly the same place every single month. No world domination was happening at our end. In fact, on more and more days it felt like surrender.

There was so much stress everywhere, it was palpable in the air. I was stressed. My team were stressed. No one was happy working at our office. Our clients were on perpetual roller coasters as to whether or not they were happy. Steve and I had to have some difficult conversations. Were we out of our minds when we thought that this could work? What did we do wrong? What were we doing wrong? Do we just give up and shut it down? We knew that we couldn't keep this going. We were still not drawing a dime out of the business and it was sucking the life out of both of us. If you've not been there, it's pretty tough to keep motivated and excited about a business that isn't providing you with any kind of a return at all. Nil. Nada. And no prospect in the future that there was going to be a return. I also found that both Steve and I were starting to resent our staff who WERE getting paid, which you can pretty much imagine isn't a good place to be as a boss or any kind of leader.

So it's a pretty uplifting story so far, don't you think? Have we got you motivated to just run out and start your own bookkeeping business, or any business for that matter? Probably not.

If you were to meet us today, would you ever think that this was our beginning story? Probably not. It's not really something that we talk about or share. It's certainly not something that we would have advertised to our clients or put on our website.

But chaos, thrashing about in the whitewater, was definitely where we were at.

The key is to get out of this phase as quickly as possible; otherwise you will definitely lose your sanity. This stage is the one which most startups never get through, and the one in which most of them fail. We were determined not to be one of those statistics.

More importantly, let's make sure that you aren't also!

The one critical thing to remember in all of this, is that success is not a direct line trajectory. It isn't going to be uphill, or any kind of a straight line at all. As you grow, you will slip back into one of the earlier stages, because you've created new problems that you've never encountered before. So you need to fix them. Then continue the upward ascent to the next level.

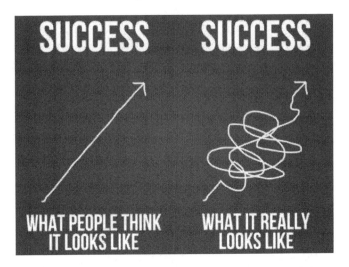

You've identified your vision. You now have some clients. You've got some money coming in. Probably not enough, but some. But lots of challenges and learnings.

Here were some of our challenges.

- Missing client deadlines
- Unhappy clients
- Losing clients
- Long days but never getting ahead - most days not even caught up
- Not profitable
- Too much rework
- Everyone doing their own thing, differently, for every client

Let's look a little deeper into all of them and see if any of these resonate with you.

Missing Client Deadlines

This is usually the first sign of things going horribly wrong. Some of these missed deadlines will be evident to you, but not your clients. Some of them your clients will catch, and you will feel horrible and try to make it right as best you can. But the worst part is when you miss one, then the next, and then you lay awake at night, every night, wondering whether you got everything done that you were supposed to today. So you start making lists so you don't forget. They could be paper lists, post it notes stuck to your monitors, or tech lists - To do apps, excel lists, word lists, calendar apps. There are a bunch of ways that you try to make sure that this doesn't happen again for that client. Or the next client.

I still remember our turning point. It was with one of our larger clients back then and we were responsible for their payroll, reconciliation pieces and sales tax returns. It was April, the peak of tax season in our part of the world. Most of our daily brainpower was focused on getting through all of the tax returns that we had to file. We were all overworked. And tired. And run down. And one of our team members got sick. (You can see where this is going, can't you?)

Everyone already had so much on their own individual plate that they did not have the capacity to pick up the workload from someone else. So you know who it was, right? Yup, it was me. Because I was the martyr in my business. If something needed to be done that required an all-nighter, I couldn't ask my team to do that; I had to do it. If I wasn't staying up all night, how could I possibly ask them to do that?

So I was pulling 16 -20 hour days and I missed something. It was inevitable. You would have thought I would see it coming. But I was head down in the work, and not looking anywhere beyond what the next thing was on my to-do list. And I had lists everywhere!! But all of those lists didn't help me and I missed filing a sales tax return for one of our clients. They owed some money and as often happens, it's the client who realized something was missed instead of us. So we did the right thing, said that it was our fault completely, and we would pick up any of the interest or penalties that were imposed on the return being filed late. When the government assessment finally arrived, it came in at $1560. Seven years later and I still remember the exact amount. I still remember having to leave the office so that I didn't break down in front of my team. I didn't have $1560. Where was I going to find another $1500 that month? But I couldn't tell the client that I couldn't afford it. The image that I had worked so hard to cultivate is that we were successful.

And anyway, it was the right thing to do, so I had to find it somewhere. I took out an advance on my credit card to pay for the penalties. But I had no choice. Credit card companies are now mandated to list how long it will take you to pay off your credit card balance if you are only making minimum payments. I think it would be something like 10 years for me to pay off that $1500 and I'd pay more in interest over that time period than the original cash advance amount I would take.

Needless to say, it wasn't a good point for me. Not only was I having to fork out money I didn't have, but I, of course, I was beating myself up for doing something so stupid. I'm smarter than that. I'm more organized than that. I should know better. And on…and on…sound familiar?

Well, let me stop you right there.

Because Steve is the one who stopped me. And you might not have a Steve in your life. You are human. Are you perfect? Heck no! Will you remember this lesson and learn something from it so that you don't repeat it? (The detail with which I've been able to describe the story should answer that question for you.)

But that was our turning point. We implemented a project management system in our office to track our deadlines. We'll go into more detail on that later.

Back to our list of where we were at.

Unhappy Clients

Of course, the logical result of missing client deadlines is unhappy clients. Not every missed deadline cost us money, but they were costing us our reputation. And we lost clients because we weren't able to hold up our promises and they got tired of hearing that "We are working on it," or "It's not ready yet, but…"

Because of the nature of who I am, I saw every unhappy client as a direct personal reflection upon myself. I know that's wrong. But it is certainly where I was at that time.

"Give yourself a break. Stop beating yourself up! Everyone makes mistakes, has setbacks and failures. You don't come with a book on how to get it right all the time. You will fail sometimes, not because you planned to, but simply because you're human. Failure is part of creating a great life. " - Les Brown

Long Days But Never Getting Ahead

The more things I was worried about missing, the longer I worked. And working longer was certainly not working smarter. I wasn't more productive. I'm pretty sure that by hour 10, I wasn't productive at all. In fact, now I know that I would have been more productive had I stopped then rather than kept going. Because it was at hour 11 and 12 where I made mistakes. Then I had to spend time I didn't have later on to fix them.

But knowing that you're working a long day, and also knowing that you are actually still going to be behind isn't a good place to be. It can really kill your motivation.

Not Profitable

Working really hard but then seeing a big pay day can sometimes get you through the next week. At least in the short term. But it's so much harder when you aren't even making money for your business, let alone none for yourself.

I was also a control freak, so the only person who did the bookkeeping for AIS Solutions was me. Yes, that is not a typo. I was supposed to be the CEO of my company and I was still doing my own bookkeeping. So, as you might expect, my bookkeeping came after all of the client work that had to be done. The only piece that I did fairly regularly was our invoicing, because we were flat rate. We had a couple of hourly clients still grandfathered in from the Aurora International days, and that invoicing was sporadic. We would go months without issuing an invoice, and then of course when we finally did, it would be big and so the client would call and say they couldn't afford it…another vicious endless loop!

Too Much Rework

I've already touched on this. For all that we were working long hours, we weren't doing a great job in those late night hours, and so would end up having to check things over and over and over again. Or we would catch mistakes at crucial month end or sales tax filing times. There was a lot of time being spent doing work for a second or third time. And, obviously when you are flat fee this doesn't help your efficiency and certainly not your profitability.

Everyone Doing Their Own thing, Differently, For Every Client

Of all of the things I've listed so far, this is probably the biggest one. This was also the one that caused me the most sleepless nights because I knew that it was the hardest hurdle to overcome.

Everything I've listed so far was pretty much about me. Things that I was doing, how I was feeling, things that I had control over. This last one was about my team…how they were doing things, and how inconsistent things were from one client to the next.

Also, when one of our team members got sick during tax time and I jumped in, I had no idea what she had done or how she was doing things, and so was always calling her, while she was sick, so that I could ask her questions!!

So does any of that resonate with you and your current situation? Hopefully I've not depressed you by sharing our situation, but instead shown you that you aren't alone. We all are either there now, or have been there. The key is that it can change. You can change it. And my hope is that you will be able to look back upon it from a much a better place, and a place of more peace.

> **STEVE'S SLANT**
> As much as this was a very difficult period for Juliet, it was one of the most frustrating for me. But, for very different reasons than her. You see, like any loving spouse, you want to support and help your partner when things are not going well.
> But, I wasn't just her spouse. I was also her business partner. So, why didn't I just jump right in and help with the workload? Easy. I didn't have the skillset. I am not a bookkeeper. I am not an accounting professional. Plus I was still running my own business. Whenever I did try to help it usually took Juliet even

> more time since she had to explain to me "how" to do it in the software. Frustration grew. I was feeling very helpless and hopeless, neither of which work well with my personality. Still hanging on to that rollercoaster.

The Turning Point

So let's just do a quick recap of where we were at in mid-2011.

- Missing client deadlines
- Unhappy clients
- Losing clients
- Long days but never getting ahead - most days not even caught up
- Not profitable
- Too much rework
- Everyone doing their own thing, differently, for every client

Needless to say, that wasn't a good place for me to be. I still felt like it was my name on the door, and all of this poor work that we were producing was causing me more angst than I could ever imagine. My answer to solve that problem was that nothing left the office without me looking at it first. NOTHING. You can pretty much imagine how well that worked out.

I then became the bottleneck for everything. I was working silly hours, and never making any progress. I hated what I was doing. I was thinking that I could do it all better and faster myself, so why was I paying all these staff members when I wasn't even taking a pay cheque?

It was not a good place for me, for my company, for my staff, for my clients or for my partner and husband.

So Steve and I decided that either something fundamental needed to change, or we needed to close the doors. What we had was not sustainable, but we didn't have any idea what it was we had to change. We bounced around the idea of a business coach, but our first reaction was - why? Why would we hire a business coach? We have so much business experience between the two of us. We are both smart people. We know what we need to do. But we also knew that we weren't doing it. So we leaped.

Enter Dan Holstein, ActionCoach Extraordinaire. (We didn't know about the "extraordinaire" part at the beginning.) He saved us. Literally. Sure, we did the work, but he was the one who showed us what we needed to do to save us from ourselves.

BNI® referral slip

Date: August 10, 2011
From: Juliet Aurora
To: Dan Holstein
Referral: AIS Solutions
(●) Inside ( ) Outside
( ) Given your card (✓) Wants Contact With BNI Member
Address:
Referred Person's Initials: A
Telephone: 905-333-9637
Email:
Comments: Connected already
re: New business

Changing the Way the World Does Business

We thought you might enjoy this image. At the time we connected with Dan, Juliet and he were in the same BNI chapter. (For those of you who don't know, BNI is an international networking organization with over 200,000 members worldwide.) This is a copy of the referral slip that Juliet had given to Dan asking to speak with him about his coaching services. We thought it was pretty awesome that Dan had held onto this and gave it to us when he heard we were writing the book.

So back to the leap. And it was a scary leap. We were already pouring funds into the business to keep it afloat, and there was no cash flow left over to pay for a business coach. So we went on faith, or were just plain crazy - take your pick - and pulled money out of our retirement savings to pay for Dan. The business coach was going to cost us $2600 a month, and we would meet with him one hour a week, every week. It was certainly $2600 we didn't have at that time, but it was either that, or close the doors. And neither Steve, nor myself, handle failure well.

This would probably be a book all unto itself. IF there was one fundamental thing that working with Dan taught us, and which created the shift for everything we did - it was that our mindset needed to change. Before anything else would change, we needed our mindset to change. And believe me when I tell you, that isn't easy.

So our first shift was understanding what a business actually is. I think this is important enough that I will repeat the definition, and it might not be what you expect - "A commercial, profitable enterprise that runs without you."

Whoa…..what? Let me repeat that.

"A commercial, profitable enterprise that *runs without you.*"

Can your business run without you? If not, then you've not created a business, but a job for yourself. And that is exactly what we had done. With me putting in place the mandate that nothing left the office without me seeing it first, there was no way that the business could run without me. If anything, I had inserted myself right, smack into the centre, so that there was no way it would ever run without me.

> **STEVE'S SLANT**
> Deciding to hire a business coach was huge for me. I had been a successful entrepreneur for over 25 years, owning several different businesses. How could I possibly need a coach now?
> However, It was working with Dan, that I learned a very hard lesson. In retrospect, I had actually *never* owned a successful business. What I had done in each business was to create a successful job for myself which is a completely different matter. Here is what I came to learn is the definition of a business - "a profitable enterprise that can operate without you." And I knew deep inside that none of my previous businesses could operate successfully on an ongoing basis without my regular presence. That is not to stroke my own ego. That is a fact. Each new business had been my way of simply creating a new job for me...not a viable business.

What We Learned

The first step in working with our coach was to complete a business questionnaire which focused on key areas of our business, like sales, marketing, processes, cash flow, profitability, team, and also key areas of our personal life like balance, the future and leadership. The questionnaire was designed to identify what areas of our life we were currently happy with, and which ones needed work, as well as identify which ones needed the most work. So I thought "Great!" This will tell us the starting place. Unfortunately, everything came back with scores under 5 out of 10, so I must admit I felt very defeated as to how much had to be done. Once we understood, I mean really understood, that some fundamental things needed to change, I felt overwhelmed with all of the things that had to be altered.

"Don't wish it was easier. Wish you were better. Don't wish for less problems. Wish for more skills. Don't wish for less challenges. Wish for more wisdom. " - Jim Rohn

---

But where there's a will, there's a way. We sat down and went through a vision exercise. I'm sure that you've heard the phrase, "If you don't know where you are going, how will you know when you get there?"

In one year, what did I want my business and my life to look like? At that time, my most important priority was working less hours and getting paid from the business. Sounds easy enough, doesn't it? Two things. How hard could that be?

I'm going to fast forward here to nine months later. In April of 2012, nine months after we had started working with Dan, Steve and I went on a two-week, completely disconnected vacation. Yes, you read that correctly. Two weeks (not one!) and completely disconnected - no phones (other than our kids' calls), no laptops, no emails, no nothing. So, is it possible? Yes! Is it easy? No! Could we have done it without help? Absolutely not!

Let's dive in now and I'll tell you how we did it. Perhaps you are better students than Steve and I, and can do it even faster.

Organize The Chaos

One of our starting points for changing things and allowing me to pull back the ridiculous controls I had put in place, was that we needed to create a system of sorts.

"Three Rules of Work: Out of clutter find simplicity; From discord find harmony; In the middle of difficulty find opportunity." - Albert Einstein

Our first step was to implement a project management system.

This is the fall of 2011 and there were no accounting or bookkeeping specific project management systems available out there unlike today when there are a multitude of choices.

So we went with a company called 37 Signals. This would give us two things for our business - a Customer Relationship Management tool (CRM) - Highrise, which would allow us to track the leads that were coming in, and a Project Management system - Basecamp - which would allow us to create task lists for our clients to fix the "ball dropping" that was happening. We were finding a place to get everything out of everyone's individual heads and make the processes available for everyone. Did I mention that I was a control freak? I'm sure I did somewhere. The purpose of this project management system was also so that I could go to a single place and see where everyone was at with all of our clients. That way, we could see problems before they arose, and get out ahead of them rather than putting out the fires with watering cans afterwards.

We stuck with 37 signals and Basecamp for three years, until the spring of 2014 when we migrated to Teamwork, which we still use to this day.

> **STEVE'S SLANT**
> We are often asked why we don't use one of the more well-known Practice Management tools now available to our industry. It certainly isn't because they are not good. From everything I have seen they are mostly great products.
>
> Personally, I had never been a big fan of Basecamp so I found and began using Teamwork for my own online marketing and web development business several years earlier and we loved it. It took me until the spring of 2014 to convince Juliet that we needed to move AIS Solutions to Teamwork.
>
> Although Juliet was very reluctant at first because it was going to be a huge job moving everything over and re-learning a new tool for the entire team, it was the right move and Teamwork has been an integral part of our systems and processes ever since.

So let's start with what we wanted to track with our new Practice Management tool - Basecamp.

1. **Clients** - Seems pretty basic, don't you think? But in actuality, there wasn't one central place that all of the contact information for our clients could be found. All of our bookkeepers had the contact information stored in their own Outlook and there wasn't a single place to look. So that was the first step.

2. **Client Deadlines** - This was the second piece that we started populating. When was their year end? How frequently did we process payroll for them? How frequently did we file their sales tax returns? When did they have cheque runs? All of this information went into a calendar in Basecamp that allowed us (me) to look in a single place and know how many sales tax returns were due that month.

3. **Client Communication** - We implemented the process that all client communication could be found in a single place. All of it. Basecamp had the feature (and Teamwork does as well), that the project management program is bcc'd on all email communication to a client. This again allowed other members of our team to step in if needed and know where things got left off with the client. As an added bonus, it also tended to solve the he said/she said conversations. And once again, to solve my control freak issues, I could sit with my morning tea and see what was going on with our clients the day before. (You will be pleased to know that at the writing of this book, I do have control of my control issues.)

> **STEVE'S SLANT**
> In the spirit of complete accuracy I would say that Juliet may not have complete command of her control issues but she is much better today than she was in 2011.

4. **Client Task lists** - In the beginning we were bookkeepers to all kinds of businesses in any and all industries. QuickBooks, Sage, Business Visions, PCLaw, proprietary software, industry specific software ... It didn't matter. If it was a piece of accounting software, we would offer to support it for our clients. We also offered all different kinds of service levels: weekly, bi-weekly, monthly, quarterly, and annual bookkeeping. We would do your books whenever you wanted us to. We were also a tax preparation firm at that time, so we did personal and corporate taxes for clients. It was very much like in my early days of Aurora International Services, where if it had to do with numbers, I would take the job. Needless to say with all of the different service offerings we had, we needed a place to list what we did for which client. Which software were we using? How often did we do things? What did we do for them? That is what we started to build out in our client specific task lists.

Sounds easy, doesn't it? Create those four things in Basecamp and we'd be good to go! Not that easy, but it was doable. As I mentioned before, Basecamp wasn't specific to our industry so we had to customize a lot to get it working for us. It was basically a roadmap that we had to build ourselves, and to be honest, when we started, we didn't even know what we wanted. It took a couple of tries before we got it right. Sometimes we caught things that needed to be corrected early on, sometimes, not so much. But we built it out. And it helped. Tremendously. It took us about nine months to build it out to where I was happy with it. To be honest, if it wasn't there, I'm not sure that I would have been able to go on that two-week disconnected vacation I talked about earlier. Having Basecamp in place allowed me to feel confident that nothing would fall through the cracks while I was away.

LESSONS LEARNED:

1. Sometimes you have to take one step back so you can begin moving forward.
2. As long as everyone is paddling in the same direction you can get through any whitewater

3. We all need help. No matter how smart you are. No matter how much experience you have. Hire a coach or find a mentor. You will not regret it.

THE KNINJA WAY

3 ORANGE BELT
– CALMING SEAS (2012)

Orange Belt: An orange belt is starting to feel some progress while still seeking knowledge.

"It always seems impossible until it's done." - Nelson Mandela

Let's talk a little bit more about some of the changes that happened over the first nine months of working with Dan that helped us in taking that two-week disconnected vacation.

There were probably two things that had the biggest impact.

#1 - We stopped preparing taxes. We narrowed our focus and made the decision to no longer prepare any personal or corporate taxes and concentrate on the bookkeeping, controllership, training and system conversion sides of the business. I'm making it sound really easy, aren't I? I'm making it sound as though we woke up one morning, said "no more taxes," and voila, we were out of the tax business. Not at all. There were discussions. There were debates. There was a lot of wine consumed. I mean, bottles and bottles of wine. If you remember where we were financially, and then think about us giving away revenue, it may help you understand the angst that was going along with this decision.

But personally, I hated taxes. I hated doing them, hated thinking about them, and especially hated what the months of March and April (the main tax season in Canada) did to our team. Then there was the impact that preparing taxes had on our bookkeeping clients. The clients who were loyal to us for 12 months of the year were pretty much ignored for the two months of tax season. So as we focused on providing better, more consistent service to them, we realized that either we needed to establish a separate tax division, or we needed to stop offering the service. We chose the latter.

Getting out of the tax business was the beginning of our specialization, or finding our focus. It actually was moving us closer to our niche, although we didn't know it at the time.

> **STEVE'S SLANT**
> Juliet is downplaying what a tough decision that was. It was probably one of the toughest decisions we made early on in our relationship with Dan. It was also one of the best. Once we made the leap, we wished that we had made it sooner, because we had some unintended results from this decision. Our bookkeeping business grew and very quickly made up the lost revenue from the tax side. How, you ask? We were no longer competing with the CA (now CPA) firms in our area. We created alliances with these firms where we would refer tax clients and they would refer bookkeeping business. So by giving up a $1,000 tax return client, we gained a monthly recurring revenue stream in its place. Makes perfect sense. Hindsight is 20/20. So the moral of the story is that you CAN get bigger even though you are reducing your service offerings.

#2 - We focused on building our team and having some fun with the people who were fundamental to our success. The first thing we did was choose a charitable event that we could all rally around.

I'm not sure that we really thought through our first team charity event, as we were all just excited to be doing something new. What we chose was put on by the Canadian Cancer Society and was called the 24

Hour Relay for Life. Yes. The title was accurate. It was a 24 hour relay. Like I said, not sure we weren't too ambitious for our first event, but it was awesome. It was a family event, and really started to develop our team as the AIS family, as we all got to know each other a little more than just within the business walls.

Our 2013 charity event was a little less intense and definitely not affected by rain. Folks who have only known Steve for the past few years may not know that he has not always had the fashionable hair style he currently possesses.

The team rallied behind and supported the St. Baldrick's Foundation, which is a non-profit organization that raises money to help find cures for children with cancer. The annual event is to get your head shaved to help raise money. Here is Steve getting his new style which he has stayed with ever since.

LESSONS LEARNED:

1. You can achieve greater success by offering fewer services
2. Having the right team is everything. Without that your business will go nowhere.

4 GREEN BELT
– SAILING ALONG (2013)

Green Belt: A green belt continues to build a little momentum and refine essential skills.

Things began to run smoothly as we jumped off the roller coaster for a while.

It really is interesting how our businesses, like our lives, seem to go through cycles. As fans of Jim Rohn, we were often reminded of his comparison of business cycles to nature's seasons. The season we had been in during the course of the last chapter might be considered spring, where we had planted the seeds towards success (becoming intentional about building our culture, removing ourselves from the tax preparation service). And then summer came, where we began to reap the rewards of that seeding.

But after the summer comes fall and then winter, where the challenges and the strength of our entrepreneurial drive are put to the test.

> **STEVE'S SLANT**
> I am a huge fan of Jim Rohn; some might even use the term "groupie." I have all of his books and audio recordings. In his book *The Seasons of Life* he talks in great detail about the parallels between life (and business) and the seasons. He details how the seasons will change without fail and what we can do to utilize each season to reap the greatest rewards. What it is we need to do in one season, in order to ensure success in another season? In many ways I also think it helps us to understand why that illustration of success is not just one straight line upward. I often use this four season analogy in my own life to better ground myself. When we are enjoying a particularly good period of business I quietly remind myself to enjoy it, but make sure we are planning for the upcoming fall and winter. So far, it has served me well.

But before we entered our own season of fall, we started to receive some external recognition. In 2013, we were now a fairly strong, productive team of six. There was connection and cohesion and camaraderie among our team members. I was still working some longer hours than I wanted, but not all evenings and weekends were filled with work and we were finally taking a regular pay cheque from the business. (Believe me that was a BIG milestone!)

In this year, we were nominated for a Small Business Excellence Award by our local Chamber of Commerce. We were interviewed by a member of the awards committee and you basically have a half hour to tell them why you're so special, what you do differently, and why you should be the one to get this award for your category. There were some questions that they came with to the interview, but honestly, it is your ability to weave into those questions the answers that you really want them to hear that makes the difference.

Talking about myself was not my strength. Talking about how great we are, was definitely not my strength! Was it because I didn't believe it? Not at all. It was mostly because I was taught early on by my parents that you didn't brag about your accomplishments. You work hard. You accomplish things.

That's just the way it is. Telling everyone, or shouting it from the rooftops was just not something that you did.

And remember that overachiever sister I mentioned

before? Well, whatever things I accomplished growing up, she had already won, earned, or done, so it was never really that big a deal. But I digress; this isn't meant to be a book about my deep, dark childhood hang-ups.

Let's go back to the Chamber of Commerce Award. Needless to say, I wasn't great at raving about us. Thankfully I had Steve in my corner. He's always been my biggest supporter and cheerleader and never had a problem telling anyone and everyone how and why we were so awesome.

When it was announced that we were one of the three finalists in the small business category, you can't even imagine how stunned I was. And Steve's response was "of course we did." That pretty much sums it all up as to how differently our brains work.

Our whole team was so excited for us. It was really a huge deal for us, and so we decided to take the whole team to the Awards Gala in April 2013. It was a glitzy affair and our team was talking about dresses and shoes for weeks! (Steve may correct me and say that it was months, not weeks). We closed the office early so everyone had time to get ready and I had more time to rehearse my acceptance speech and try to get my nerves under control.

Unfortunately, we didn't win that year, nor did we win

the following year, when we once again made the finalist list. It actually was the third year of making it to that short list that we won. The running joke was that I was going to be like Susan Lucci who played Erica on *All My Children* and was nominated 19 times for an Emmy, until she finally won in 1999.

Here we are with our coach, Dan, in 2015 when we

won the Chamber of Commerce Small Business Excellence Award.

But at that first gala in 2013, I don't know who was more disappointed that we lost - me or my team. We received a plaque for making it to the finals, but the most important thing that came out of it was our common goal. It really is true that a common purpose is so powerful for your team. So the strength of all of our relationships were forged that night. That, and our tradition of having a picture taken of all of us in our fancy shoes, was born that night.

There was also another surprise for me the next day at the office. We were having our regular team meeting and I was asked to please read for them my acceptance speech. They felt that I should still read my speech despite not being awarded a trophy by the Chamber of Commerce since we definitely were winners.

I was speechless. I was supposed to be the leader of that organization. I was supposed to rally the troops and keep the positive attitude in the office, but with that single, simple request, I was humbled. I was touched more than they would probably ever know that there was so much concern for me and my feelings.

LESSONS LEARNED:

1. Even when you lose, you can win.

2. You reap what you sow. Never believe that the leadership you show won't be reflected back at you when you least expect it and possibly when you need it the most.

Our Team

So I've spoken a lot about what we were doing wrong, and what we learned about our systems and processes and what needed to happen. But I've not really spoken about the most important part of our entire business - our team. So let's spend a little bit of time there.

I mentioned earlier in the book that a big part of Neville's time was spent hiring people. And we did it pretty much the same way that most business owners do - place an ad, read resumes, conduct interviews, go by your gut, cross your fingers and select a candidate. We also found that in that first 12 months we went through a lot of bookkeepers. And I mean a lot. We found that many of the bookkeepers looked amazing on paper, but not so much in real life situations. Because we also had little to no systems or checkpoints in place to ensure that the work was being done correctly, we usually didn't find out about mistakes until they became a big mess. And the messes tended to be discovered after we let someone go. You already know how I was feeling about having to check everything that left the office, so imagine what it was like when we were changing staff so frequently.

We also encountered two other challenges with our high turnover and the revolving door of bookkeepers.

1. Our clients went through some pain every time they started with someone new. It also hurt our credibility when we kept introducing them to their new lead bookkeeping contact.

2. We never got ahead. This was a big one for us. As you know whenever you hire someone, there is a great deal of lead time before they are up to speed. And during that lead time, someone else is having to pick up some slack. With such high turnover we never really got ahead with the whole team being efficient and productive at the same time.

I guess there was also a third challenge for us. It's tough to bring camaraderie and a sense of team to the office if the people in the team are always changing!

So we introduced testing. I got tired of relying on someone's resume where they said they were "experts" at everything and had 10 years of experience. If their resume was truthful, they would have no problems passing my tests. If they had embellished their resume then we would know before we ever invested a dime in training them.

So what did we test? There were three tests that every candidate had to go through.

#1 - A Bookkeeping Fundamentals test. If we take the software away from you, do you understand the basics of bookkeeping? What is an asset, a liability, income or an expense? What does a balance sheet represent versus an income statement and why do businesses need both? And of course, the debit and credit knowledge was absolutely required.

#2 - A QuickBooks/Sage software test. Those were the two primary pieces of software we were using at the time, so we created a series of exercises that applicants had to perform in the software while we watched. They included how to enter a bill, pay a bill, create a sales invoice, reconcile a bank account, and run a report. It wasn't designed to trick anyone, or give them random questions that no one would ever know. The test was designed to see the extent of their working knowledge of the software.

#3 - An Excel test. At the time, Excel was still a big part of what we did, so we needed to ensure that the bookkeepers knew how to use it. Again, we weren't looking for Advanced Excel features like Macros or pivot tables. It was how to create a sum formula, or format cells and customize reports downloaded from QuickBooks.

As we started to implement this round of tests, the results were amazing and amazing from a couple of different viewpoints. In order for us to offer the person a position we had determined that they had to get a minimum of 80% on all three tests. There were no exceptions being made. As we said, the tests weren't complicated or tricky; they were testing for fundamentals.

1st gain - We eliminated so many people without having to hire them first. It was actually amazing how for some of the people we thought that the test was just going to be a formality, because we were sure they were the one. But they weren't. The test results showed us that.

2nd gain - We found that the candidates were a little more honest with us, knowing that they were going to be tested. An expert in QuickBooks and Sage on their resume? Then they have to take both tests, and they would then confess that they hadn't used Sage in eight years, or that they only studied QuickBooks in school, but hadn't actually used it you get the drift.

3rd gain - We started to get some momentum with hiring better people, at least from a skills level.

We introduced the testing process early on, but expanded upon it with a more automated and streamlined hiring process shortly after.

Culture

We now felt we were getting some traction with our business. The work was getting done and getting done correctly. I was a little more relaxed as I had more confidence in what we were producing for our clients. It all seemed to be going well.

Then we realized something. The office had gotten quieter. There was less conversation among our staff and there seemed to be some tension in the air on some days. But why? Everything seemed to be running better. Our clients were happier. I was happier. (Which means Steve was happier.) But tension was there, just under the surface.

"If you want to build a ship don't herd people together to collect wood. Don't assign them tasks and work, but rather teach them to long for the endless immensity of the sea." - Jonathan Rosenberg

---

It took us a while to figure it out, but as we grew the team, we obviously had more varied personalities in the space. We weren't a huge office, so if you didn't get along with someone, it was pretty evident and hard to avoid them.

It was something that our coach pointed out to us one day when he came for our session. I'm not sure that we would have been able to put our finger on it because we were so deep into it every day. But it was one of our team. She was an awesome bookkeeper, one of the smartest on our team who always met all of her deadlines. But it was her attitude that was so negative and "anti-team" that it really permeated everything. So we decided to let her go.

Such a simple sentence, but honestly not a simple decision. I was finally at a place where I was starting to get some confidence in the work we were doing. And she really was one of the best bookkeepers that we had. But if no one *wanted* to come to work, then we would pretty much lose everyone else if she stayed.

When we let her go, she even said to us "But how can you let me go, I'm your best bookkeeper?"

The next morning we let the rest of the staff know, and the immediate change in the air was evident. It was like this huge weight had been lifted off the rest of the staff and they started to become a team. Up until now, in our business they were employees or staff. But from that moment on, they became a team and we realized how important the personality and the attitude of our team members was to the overall feeling of the team and the office. From that point onward, we began focusing on the fit of applicants and less on their skills. It was an eye-opening moment for Steve and me.

As we noticed this change coming over the team we also realized that the culture in our office was going to develop. Either we could drive its direction, or the team would. But it would happen.

So we changed our hiring process. The additions to our hiring process were initially introduced to us by Dan and ActionCoach and we evolved it to better suit our own business. The purpose of modifying our process was twofold:

To save time for the people conducting the process - which at the time was Steve and me.

To improve the efficiency and effectiveness of selecting the right candidates.

We did this primarily through automation and had the potential candidates filter themselves out of our selection process on their own by providing them with tasks to complete that required no effort on our part. We did leave the testing process in place, but it was conducted only when we got to the short list.

(We could write another book just on what our hiring process looks like and what it did for us, including the autoresponders and group interview, but if you want more information just visit our website https://www.kninja.net and look under resources for the program - Hiring the Kninja Way.)

So now that we knew we had to focus on our culture and be more cognizant of the values and personality of our team, not just their skills, a couple of other things began to happen for us.

Who knew that it was all so connected?

Remember that two week, completely disconnected vacation I mentioned earlier? Well, before we went away, we told our then four-person team that we were going on vacation. They nodded their heads, thinking it was going to be like every other vacation, where basically we were still available, doing everything we always did, with just our bodies in a different country and our laptops perhaps plugged into a different voltage outlet.

Then we told them that we actually were going to disconnect for this vacation, and wouldn't be reachable - FOR ANYTHING.

If the office was on fire, don't call us, call the fire department and the insurance company - just not us. They all looked at each other, not sure if they had heard us properly.

This may not seem like such a big deal. And if you've been able to do this already, then kudos to you! You have to remember, this is also the same person, who not that long ago, wouldn't let them send a single thing out of the office without me looking at it first. But we told them that they knew what had to be done. There were checklists and calendars in place of all the upcoming deadlines. We told them to handle whatever came their way. We told them that we trusted them. (To be honest, it was terrifying for me! But they certainly wouldn't have known it from the words coming out of my mouth.)

So we left. We relaxed, at least eventually.

We actually had some downtime and time to spend as husband and wife, not just business partners. We were tempted to call the office "just to check in," but heard our coach's voice on the beach with us, reminding us that we were creating a business. "A commercial, profitable enterprise <u>that runs without us.</u>" Those last four words were the bane of my existence for many years.

> **STEVE'S SLANT**
> :-)

Then we came back. Relaxed. Rejuvenated. With a tan (deeper tan for me) and re-energized to build our business. Without all of the day-to-day noise filling our brains, we were also able to look more objectively at our business. We considered what needed to be fixed, and what we wanted to do next. And that was just the change in us.

The change in our team was even more magical. As would be expected, some challenges arose while we were away. But the team rallied together and handled them. I know! What a concept! When I wasn't there, micromanaging everything, looking over their shoulders and making decisions for them, they all stepped up and took care of <u>everything</u>.

"Coming together is a beginning. Keeping together is progress. Working together is success." - Henry Ford

---

So, as much as that vacation had originally been for us, it taught us something important about our team. It taught us that we had truly built a *team,* not just a group of people coming together under one roof to collect a pay cheque.

We also learned that by empowering our team, they were happier. And guess who's happier when the team is happier? Our clients.

So three fundamental changes were implemented as a result of that time away:

#1 - I stopped micromanaging. I stopped being the gateway for everything but clearly communicated, that *if* there was a problem, I needed to hear about it from *them*, not from the client.

#2 - We made a more conscious effort to focus on our culture and started the first iteration of our Wall of Culture. (More about this in the next section).

#3 - We no longer referred to everyone in our office as staff. From that day forward it was team members only. Even to this day, nowhere will you see or hear the word "staff" or "employee" on anything in our office.

> **STEVE'S SLANT**
> A personal observation. If you want to build a great team...make sure you always call them a team...when they are present and when they are not. They are not employees. They are not staff members. They are people and they are part of your team and the reality is that without them you have no business. (I will now step off my soapbox.)

Our Wall of Culture

So what is our Wall of Culture? In its simplest form, it is a visual representation of the things that we value as individuals and as an organization.

> "Corporate culture matters. How management chooses to treat its people impacts everything - for better or for worse." - Simon Sinek

We could have chosen any number of ways to represent these points of culture, but chose to do so with a single word and an image that represented the word.

So what were our points of culture going to be? For them to be meaningful, they couldn't be dictated or decided by Steve and me. If they were, the only people that it would hold any meaning for would be us. And that's not what we wanted, because we were a team.

STEVE'S SLANT

Like Juliet I felt it was very important that the team help to develop our Wall of Culture. However, I also felt very strongly that it was important that no matter how the words evolved on the wall it was critically important that the wall began with our own core beliefs and that revolved around "Above and Below the Line." As you can see from the image it is the centerpiece of the wall as everything else developed from it.

Above the Line/Below the Line

The Above the Line/Below the Line was the representation of a phrase that we adapted from our coach, Dan.

It basically asks the question as to whether or not you are living your life Above or Below the Line.

And here's what that means:

You should always be striving to live "Above the Line" and that means you take OWNERSHIP of your decisions and actions, you are ACCOUNTABLE for those actions and you take RESPONSIBILITY for them. In staying above the line you will develop trust with the people around you - your fellow team members, your clients, your friends and your family.

Just as important, it means you are always trying to avoid being "Below the Line" by BLAMING others when things don't go right, making EXCUSES for mistakes you make and DENYING any responsibility. Obviously, if you spend most of your time below the line it will be very difficult, if not impossible, to develop any kind of trust.

Ownership
Accountability
Responsibility

Blame
Excuses
Denial

The first time we heard this concept, it really resonated with both of us.

It made perfect sense in our business lives, but it also made sense in our personal lives. When we first started on the journey of living by this concept, we realized how much we actually were living Below the Line, and either denying what was wrong, or making excuses for things. And it is only when you are aware of something that you are doing that you then are given the ability to change the behaviour.

Steve and I both wanted to change this behaviour and live our lives "Above the Line". So we started calling each other out when one or the other of us ventured Below the Line. It was said respectfully, but it was brought to our attention when we started to drift. Interestingly enough, it became such a regular part of our vernacular that our daughter learned it as well. I still remember the first time she called out her grandmother for saying something that was Below the Line.

As Steve and I wanted to ensure that the environment at AIS was not only a positive one, but one where the team took ownership and responsibility for their role in the organization, it seemed only fitting that the centre of our Wall of Culture would be "Above the Line and Below the Line." It has now been five years since we implemented that first picture and you will hear others call their teammates (and us) out for saying something "Below the Line." So it has definitely worked.

So the first words on our Wall of Culture was actually a phrase and was chosen by us.

We then started adding two new words every month. But all of the additional words were chosen and decided upon by our team.

Actually, decided is probably the wrong word. Debated. The words were debated upon by our team as to what was most important to them, and why.

This process continued until we had an additional seven words. So it took us about four months to build out our wall. It probably would have taken longer except that there were two words going up every time, except for the last. (And as a side note, here's why there were two - I have this "thing" about symmetry, and putting only one word up at a time would have made the wall asymmetrical for an entire month at a time and would have kept me awake at night.)

(Additional Side Note - I recently learned that this dislike of asymmetry is a trait that runs prevalent in our industry! I honestly was so excited when someone posted on a Facebook group their dislike of asymmetry and how it drove them crazy. The number of people that this resonated with was amazing - and comforting - to me. I've only been razzed by my family and friends for my need of symmetry, that it was comforting to find a tribe of people just like me.)

But I digress. Back to our Wall of Culture. It was about four months for the whole wall to be built out. We were stuck at five pictures for a couple of weeks since we couldn't get agreement on what the next pair of words would be, but we finally did. These are the words that we ended up with as chosen by our team.

- OWNERSHIP
- EXCELLENCE
- BALANCE
- INTEGRITY
- GRATITUDE
- EDUCATION
- TEAMWORK

And of course, Above & Below the Line in the centre.

Here is a picture of the final wall of culture.

This collection of photos held the place of honour on the wall behind the open area of desks in our office so that my team saw it each and every day. When we relocated offices later on, it became the main wall of our boardroom. It also served as a reminder for when someone wasn't sure which decision to make: Did it uphold and stay true to all of the points of culture on our wall?

Don't get me wrong. Just because we built out this wall, and had these words displayed every day, there were times that we lost our way. There were times that our culture was the afterthought, not the one front and centre. We're human after all. We're certainly not perfect. We are usually smart, but sometimes we're slow and the path to success is not a straight line.

As we promised at the outset of this book - we would share not only what worked, but mistakes we made, because both are equally important. And we never want the perception to be that we are perfect, or that our journey was a smooth one. That poses the risk that it would also make you feel bad, as though you are doing something wrong, which is also likely furthest from the truth.

One mistake we made was that we didn't react quickly enough when a client was continually rude to one of our team members.

You know how hard it is to get new clients. Especially at the beginning. I probably don't need to tell you how in those early days of building a business, we took every client that came our way. We weren't discerning at all - industry, software, requirements, frequency, it didn't matter. (Note: We didn't even understand the word "niche" at this point.)

If they wanted our services, we agreed. If anything, we were thankful. I know. Think about that. *We* were thankful that someone wanted to pay us so that we could help them and take care of their financial data so they could grow their business.

Sounds crazy when you see the words down on paper in front of you. Do you think that we saw value in the services we were providing our clients? No, I think not. But that is another chapter all unto itself. What we found out was that one of our clients would consistently yell at one of our team members. There was some talk that I'd "kind of" heard about how they didn't much like him and he as a PITA (Pain in the A**) client. But I kind of shrugged it off because our clients were mostly pretty good and if we had one that wasn't perfect, I could live with that.

But there were a couple of problems going on here:

#1 - I didn't have a full understanding of *how* bad this client was. I had swung so far in the other direction from micromanaging to disassociating myself that I didn't know. An important lesson we learned here was the big difference between delegating and abdicating. (It is a concept that has taken me a long time to master, and sometimes still forget.)

#2 - I had built the mantra among our team that our goal was "to make our clients' lives easier." But I hadn't qualified that statement with my team that it wasn't to be at *any* expense, least of all their expense.

#3 - I hadn't created the right culture with my team for someone else to tell me. Although I didn't know what was going on, the rest of the team did know, and

<u>no one</u> came forward to tell me that something needed to be done.

I'm not blaming anyone on my team, as that would be Below the Line. I was the one to blame that I didn't have a clue what was going on. I also hadn't created a team who felt that they could come to me and I would have their backs -- who didn't feel unconditionally that I would choose their side over that of the client.

I ended up finding out one day purely by accident. I was walking past one of my team members and she was so visibly upset that I asked her if she was okay. She said she was fine, but one of the other ladies said "Oh, she just got off the phone again with Brian (not his real name). I stood there for a second and thought that sounded too nonchalant, and was this a regular occurrence? It was only when I asked the right questions that I found out that this happened at least once a week, and had been going on for some time.

So two things happened that afternoon:

#1 - I called the client and gave them our 30 day notice as per our engagement agreement. When asked why, I told him that the most important thing to me was that my team was treated with respect and that I've learned that hasn't been happening so we were unable to continue providing services. I also stated that we would make the transition as smooth as possible to his new provider over the next 30 days, but if I heard that he was speaking to any of my team the way he had been, services would end immediately and we would not complete any transition.

#2 - I sat down with my team to reinforce that *I* was part of the team, that there was no client who could treat them like that as long as my name was on the door. I reminded them that one of the words on our Wall of Culture was "Integrity" and that a big part of integrity was dealing with others and our own selves with respect. And that's how they should always feel - not just from other team members, but by anyone, always. I reminded them that I couldn't fix something if they didn't tell me about it. And if the person experiencing it couldn't tell me, it was the responsibility of the rest of the "team" (another word on the wall), to look out for one another and to let me know.

I then told them that I had fired the client and we wouldn't be working with them after the 30 day notice I had to provide as laid out in our engagement letter. But that if over those 30 days there was *one* iota of disrespect, I was to be informed immediately.

The silence in the room was deafening. They couldn't believe that I had fired a client. I couldn't believe that they couldn't believe it!

It was enlightening and an eye opener for both sides.

LESSONS LEARNED:

1. Don't assume that your team considers you as part of the team unless you do something that shows them you are. Actions speak louder than words.

2. Value yourself and the services that you provide. If you don't place value on yourself, how will you expect anyone else to see your value?

3. Be intentional about your culture. If you aren't, it will develop without you.

Although it all sounds so very serious in our office, it actually isn't. In fact, we try to have a lot of fun within our four walls, as we know that so much of our lives are spent at the office. So, yes, the work needs to get done, but fun needs to be had. We celebrate birthdays, with the birthday person required to wear a silly hat, crown, glasses or sash for the day. Cupcakes are a big thing with us; as is chocolate. We also have an AIS Games Day, every Wednesday afternoon, where Juliet's Jems take on Steve's Sassy Strikers in 6 week game events like Trivial Pursuit, Pictionary, Bowling, Mini Golf, or Nerf Gun Bowling. The book would be remiss without some of those crazy pictures. Our

Facebook page has them all, if you want to see the entire collection
https://www.facebook.com/aissolutions/

THE KNINJA WAY

5 BLUE BELT
– THE SHIFT (2014)

Blue Belt: A blue belt continues a focused pursuit of knowledge in order to continue to grow and develop.

"Success breeds complacency. Complacency breeds failure. Only the paranoid survive." - Andy Grove

---

Things were going well. Business was good. Business was steady. We were growing. Not exponentially, but steadily every year.

And I was getting bored. It was a lot of the same old, same old. How true the saying of Lou Holtz, "In this world you're either growing or you're dying, so get in motion and grow." Because that's absolutely what happened. We even stopped working with Dan, our coach, because we thought that we had arrived. We figured we were done. As I'm sure you can guess, based on this not being the end of the book, we weren't actually done.

I must admit that Steve and I get bored easily. That may not be a surprising fact about Steve, but typically those who are attracted to the accounting and bookkeeping professions like routine and order, and I would have thought that I was the same. But apparently I'm not.

So we were both getting bored. I wasn't enjoying going to the office and as I've already mentioned, the energy of the leadership tends to steer the energy of the organization, so you pretty much know what the energy of AIS felt like.

But interestingly enough, although we were bored, we also weren't looking for things to make our business exciting. We weren't on the hunt to change things up. I think back to why that would be and can only attest it to one thing - FEAR.

"Courage is knowing what not to fear." - Plato

Probably not what you thought it was going to be - right?

But I'm pretty sure that's what it was. Although we weren't overly excited about what we were doing on a day-to-day basis, we finally had arrived at a point where things were stable. Stable team. Stable growth. Stable clients. Stable cash inflow. Stable pay cheque. Stable. And boring.

You already know from our story so far that it was a hard road, with a lot of sleepless nights to get here. And if we ventured down a path of changing things up, would we be putting this stability at risk? We didn't really know, and perhaps we wouldn't have risked it at all, but we didn't seem willing to chance it. We certainly were not living by the adage - "If you're not growing, you're dying" - something we definitely believe now!

Here's a good example of how closed off we were to even contemplating the idea of change.

In the spring of 2014, my Intuit District Manager, Brad Hull, asked if he and his manager could come and talk to me. Brad had been trying for some time to get me and my firm to test out their new product in Canada - QuickBooks Online (QBO), but I wasn't interested. (Remember that fear thing?)

I agreed to the meeting out of respect for my

relationship with Brad, and he and his manager, Jeff, came to visit with me at my office in Burlington. They spoke with me about QBO, and all of the great advantages it would bring. Then, for the next 45 minutes, I proceeded to tell them why I would never move from QuickBooks Desktop (QBDT) to QBO. And I didn't just say I wasn't interested now, I said NEVER. For 45 minutes…..

I still remember the two major reasons that I gave them: (I'm pretty sure that I provided them with more, but these were the two biggies, and still stand out to me today.)

#1 - I'm already in the Cloud and have all of the advantages of anytime access with our *AIS Cloud* setup.

#2 - My team and I have already invested so much time and energy in learning and perfecting our knowledge in QuickBooks Desktop. Who was going to pay for all of the additional training in QuickBooks Online so that they would know how it worked as well as they did in Desktop? Who was going to pay for all of the inefficiency that my firm was going to experience? I wasn't willing to - remember that I was now stable, and disrupting that stability wasn't even remotely on my radar.

Jeff and Brad listened to my reasons for the full 45

minutes, and were very polite about the whole thing. Not once did they mock me for my lack of vision or flexibility. Or try to convince me that I was wrong, or that I wasn't making the best decision for my business, my clients, or my team. They politely thanked me for my time (they are Canadian, after all) and left.

It wasn't until after they left that I had learned that Jeff, Brad's "manager, "was actually Jeff Cates, the President of Intuit Canada! Are you as horrified to learn that, as I was?

Because I absolutely was. But as I said, they were both so gracious about my lack of vision.

The Power Of A Conference

So apparently, "never" is about six months. That fall, I was invited by Intuit to attend the QBConnect Conference in San Jose, California. I was honoured to be included in a VIP contingent of Canadians invited to the conference, which meant that I got some behind the scenes time with some Intuit executives. Obviously, Jeff and Brad didn't hold our conversation against me, that they included me in this awesome group.

During those four days in San Jose, I got it. I understood that QBO wasn't just QBDT with anytime access, like my *AIS Cloud.* It was so much more! I learned words that I'd never associated with our industry like Apps and Ecosystems and Automation.

But the biggest takeaway from the conference? I came back excited! Excited about the possibilities. Excited about the changes that were coming in our industry. Excited about this revolutionary shift that we were on the precipice of. Now, I'm not going to turn this chapter into a QBO infomercial or sell you on the merits of attending a QBConnect Conference. All I will tell you is that if you've never attended the QBConnect Conference in San Jose before, put this book down, and go register for the next one now. Now. No, right now. Go. I'll wait. It will fundamentally change how you view your business and expand the possibilities of what your future could look like.

So, back to our story. Those four days in San Jose fundamentally shifted our direction. We returned from the conference and told our entire team that we were going to build our business with QBO. Remember my earlier observation, at the beginning of this chapter, about the personality of the accounting professional and not wanting change? Well, needless to say, our team was stunned, and not very happy.

It was understandable though. None of them had been at the conference with me. None of them had seen or heard what I had. And I was naive enough to think that my excitement was enough to carry this new mandate through my organization. It wasn't. The introduction of QBO into our business model was an uphill battle all the way.

My personality requires me to have all of the answers, and know how all of the stuff works. All the software, all the tools. That's a great quality when you're a solo entrepreneur, but not so much (as you'll see later) if you want to be a true business owner.

So, based on my personality, my natural first step was to convert the books of my own firm from QBDT to QBO. It made perfect sense. I knew my books and business better than I did any of our client books. My books were pretty straightforward - a service based business - and I was going to tell our clients how great it was, I should certainly have my own financials there - shouldn't I?

So it was myself, and my one bookkeeper, Laurie, who delved into the world of QBO first. Laurie did the bookkeeping for AIS, and had been with me since my Aurora International days. I was excited. She was not.

> **STEVE'S SLANT**
> So Juliet has just glossed over this point completely - that Laurie was doing the bookkeeping for AIS. Let me tell you how difficult a transition it was from moving the responsibility of the bookkeeping for AIS

> from under Juliet's responsibilities to one of our team. I still recall saying to her "If you are telling our clients and potential clients how great of a team we have, why can you not trust them with *our* bookkeeping?" I also recall saying it more than once. When she finally did make the leap, it wasn't easy for her, but I can attest personally as to how much better it was for her. She moved from "doing" the books, to looking at and understanding how the numbers could help us grow. As an added benefit, it's a great story to tell potential clients that we understand how hard it is to let go of the bookkeeping for your business.

As Laurie and I were delving into the world of QuickBooks Online, I pretty much heard every complaint there was about what was wrong with the program. How the Desktop version did more. Did it better. Was more stable. Made more sense. Sure, it made more sense because we knew it inside and out. We made the mistake that most people did and still do when we started using it - we expected QBO to work the same way that QBDT did, and we tried to do everything the same way in QBO that we used to in QBDT.

I'll be honest. It took Laurie and me a while to get used to it. Switching back and forth between QuickBooks Desktop, Sage 50 and QBO also didn't help us much in getting up to speed quickly.

But I was chicken. Plain and simple. I wanted to venture out into this brave new world of Apps and Ecosystems, but I didn't want to sacrifice any of the stability I'd already achieved in our business. I wanted exciting and stable. Not really a combination you hear of too often. Or at least not successfully.

After a while, I finally managed to get Laurie excited about a few things, some of the features not available in QBDT. The ability to do things automatically that were all manual before. It was when we took our monthly invoicing process from 12-14 hours per month to under a half hour, that Laurie started to get a little excited. Albeit, she was very reluctantly excited.

We then introduced our first client to QBO and the HubDoc App. We warned him in advance that he was our guinea pig and heavily discounted everything we were doing for him because it was all so new for us. There were times that it was painful learning, but he was a good sport. Thanks Daniel!

Steve and I began to look for QBO clients. Not just new clients, but actively search for clients who wanted to be using this new tool that we had discovered. It reminded us of our early AIS Cloud days, where first we had to explain what it was and how it could benefit them. But here's where we ran into the problem. We started getting them. So….what's the problem, you're probably asking. I can hear you saying to yourself,

"What is she complaining about? I'd love to get new QBO clients just because I'm looking for them."

Well, I'll tell you.

Do you remember me saying at the beginning of this chapter that things were pretty stable? And that we liked it that way? Well, a big part of that stability was because my team was looking after pretty much all of the day-to-day stuff, and had a lot of autonomy. The introduction of QBO into the mix removed some happiness from them, which directly translated into instability and unhappiness for me.

Here's how the realization that we had a problem came to me. We have a weekly team meeting on Monday afternoons. We would use the time to bring other team members up to date on our clients. I would also talk about any new clients that were coming onboard, and whose client they would become. As we started bringing on these new clients, and I would announce to my team that we got a new *QBO* client, every single set of eyes in that room would avoid looking at me. EVERY SINGLE ONE. No one wanted the QBO clients. They only wanted the Desktop clients.

I realized that if my team wasn't rowing this boat with me, we were going to sink pretty fast. I also realized that I had seen the future at QBConnect. I had become excited, but I had disregarded the need for my team to also have that enthusiasm and excitement. Quite honestly, I had disregarded their feelings. What's that saying by Richard Branson - "Take care of your team, and they'll take care of your clients?" Well, I hadn't done that. I wasn't taking care of my team.

Our Monday meetings changed format. We addressed only challenges that needed to be solved, and switched the remainder of the meeting into QBO training sessions. I prefer to call them "Excitement generating sessions." I wanted them to be as excited as I was. About QBO, about the Apps, about the automation and the possibilities.

I'll be honest, some team members resisted, and fought me all the way. I heard about the problems and the challenges and why they didn't like it. But I kept reminding myself and them to hang in there, that all of this new stuff they were learning was going to benefit them, and keep them relevant in the industry. That we were on the leading edge of this change, and sometimes the road was bumpy.

Then one day it happened. I really don't think it was "one day" and it certainly wasn't overnight, but it was probably six months after we started this training process. We were seated in our weekly meeting. I was talking about two new clients that we had signed up. One was Desktop and one was QBO. When I talked about the Desktop client, no one would meet my eyes.

All eyes were averted. No one wanted to take another Desktop client! When I talked about the QBO client, I got questions like "What apps will they be using?" "I've not used that app, can I have that client?"

I was stunned. I was happy. I had my rock star team.

"Success is no accident. It is hard work, perseverance, learning, studying, sacrifice and most of all, love of what you are doing or learning to do." - Pele

LESSONS LEARNED:

1. Don't assume that your excitement is contagious. You need to get the 'buy-in' from your team to implement change.
2. Things don't change successfully just because you said so.
3. We were reinforced as to how important continuous learning is. Learning something new got us excited about the business again and we have become avid believers of lifelong education.

6 PURPLE BELT
– CHANGING THE FOCUS (2015)

Purple Belt: A purple belt begins to make use of their acquired knowledge to evolve and strengthen.

We were still growing. We had hired a couple of new people, lost a couple of people, but ended up ahead of the game.

"All the great organizations in the world, all have a sense of why that organization does what it does." - Simon Sinek

Before I talk about how we came to the realization that another change was needed (are you seeing a pattern here?) let's talk about our team, and some of the struggles we encountered.

We had been learning over time how key the right team is when running a business. Sure, we'd always "known" it. We can't grow without people, but after being smacked in the head with a 2 x 4 a couple of times, we realized that it's not just bodies, or number of bodies that matter. It's *who* the actual people are. Not only do they have to "fit" as we talked about in an earlier chapter, but they have to buy into your "why" and the vision for the business. They have to believe not only in what you are building, but "why" you are building it. Otherwise you are only a temporary stop for them. And temporary stops can become very costly for your business. Not only from a team cohesiveness perspective, but from a client perception as well. If you've got a revolving door with your team, your clients are going to start getting antsy.

We went through that phase. As I mentioned earlier, we had gone through the phase of having a revolving door of team members when we first started. Almost five years later, we ended up back in that same place. If you recall earlier in the book on what the path to success really looks like, you'll see that it was definitely us. As you grow, problems or challenges that you think you've solved rear their ugly head once again.

Here's the picture again, in case you forgot.

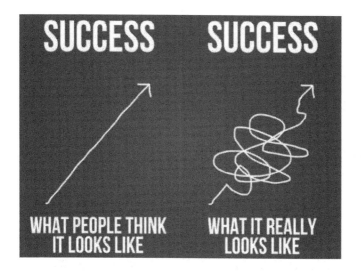

Sometimes the door didn't revolve fast enough, and we kept people around for much longer than we should have. Zappos has this great philosophy, "Hire slowly and fire quickly." It sounds so logical. And easy. But it's not. If you are like us and most other accounting/bookkeeping firms, you've got everyone busy. You usually don't hire that next person until everyone, including yourself, is overworked and stressed.

Sound familiar?

It really is a great question - we know how long it takes to find a good person. Not just a warm body, but someone who meets all the criteria we already identified above. They fit. They share your vision. Hopefully, they have some skills that will allow them to hit the ground running. It takes a while to find that person. So why then do we only start looking when we are stressed to the max? When we've reached the point that any warm body will help ease that pressure? We did that. Over and over. And over. Then we'd hire someone who wasn't right, and then hang onto them too long because "at least" they were helping a little bit.

I know. Believe me, I know. I wish that I could tell you that we've got it down perfectly now. That we now hire before we need the next person. Before my team is overwhelmed. I wish that I could tell you that for my sake, as much as yours. But we haven't perfected it. We are so much better. We do hire slower, but sometimes we still get it wrong and don't fire fast enough. Firing is hard. It is one of the toughest things for me as a business owner. I keep thinking that we can train them more, help them more, and that they'll then turn a corner. And sometimes they will. I'm not saying don't invest in your people, quite the opposite. Just invest in the right people.

As we went through this phase with the revolving door, we learned some things:

#1 - Our systems weren't strong enough. Sure we had our project management system, Teamwork. We had a project for each client with a checklist of what we had to do and what the respective deadlines were for the client. But our system wasn't strong enough to support this door that kept revolving, where the bookkeeper kept changing for our clients. Our clients kept having to repeat themselves over and over again with the idiosyncrasies that were unique to their business.

#2 - We were all over the place and needed to stop trying to be everything to everyone but narrow our focus and be better at it than anyone else out there. We couldn't be the best at everything, it just wasn't possible, and we needed to stop.

Our mission evolved to reflect this new realization - *"Our mission is to be recognized as the standard against which all other bookkeepers and bookkeeping firms are measured."*

Lofty goals don't you think? I certainly thought so, but I knew that we had it in us. This was now mid to late 2015.

In order to achieve this new vision we had mapped out for ourselves, we knew that we needed to become more consistent in our service delivery. The ever-changing cast of team members showed us that our systems and processes were too rudimentary and too generic. There were too many variations from one client to the next and one bookkeeper to another. What this meant was that when a new person started, the training and learning curve was sometimes insurmountable!

The thought of creating detailed systems for <u>all</u> of the exceptions we had in our office, and <u>all</u> of the services we provided was just overwhelming! How in the world could we possibly document EVERYTHING? It would take me years!! (Notice that my first thought was that it was me who had to do it all…..I hadn't completely let go of my control freak personality.)

Steve is always the calming force in the business. Sometimes, it's completely infuriating as to how calm he is, when I want someone to rant with me. But all in all, it's a really good quality - his calming demeanor that believes we can come up with a solution to anything.

> "Stress and worry, they solve nothing. What they do is block creativity. You are not even able to think about the solutions. Every problem has a solution." - Susan L. Taylor

We sat back and objectively looked at our business, business model, team and where we wanted to go. We revisited that vision exercise we did first when we started working with Dan. What did we want our business to look like in two years? In five years? More importantly, what did we want our lives to look like in two years? In five years?

We defined it. We documented it. We mapped it out. Then we worked backwards. Here's a synopsis of what came out of those endless discussions and copious bottles of wine we consumed:

#1 - We were trying to be all things to all people

#2 - We needed a key supervisor

#3 - We needed stronger systems and processes

We Were Trying To Be All things To All People

Even though we had scaled back on our service offerings back in 2012 by eliminating tax preparation as part of our business, and eliminating some accounting software platforms that we would support, we now knew that we had to refine it even further. With the introduction of QuickBooks Online, we were supporting three pieces of software - QuickBooks Online, QuickBooks Desktop and Sage. With the speed at which things were changing, we couldn't possibly become the expert in all three. There weren't enough hours in the day, and our team wasn't big enough that we could create segregated software teams. So we made the decision to remove Sage as a software choice, as well as focus on QBO as our main accounting platform. We weren't anywhere near as hard-nosed as when we exited out of the tax business by immediately removing those clients, but made the decision to only accept QBO clients going forward, and that within 12 months we would stop taking on new QuickBooks Desktop clients as well. Those clients who didn't want to, or couldn't, make that transition with us, would be phased out. Sure, we could have cut them off cold turkey, but to be perfectly honest, I wasn't prepared to take that many steps backwards on our monthly recurring revenue, when we were finally at a stable place. So we were much more conservative with this transition.

We also realized that we were doing too many different things in different ways for clients. There were just too many exceptions "for just this client" for us to ever create scalable, consistent processes. That too, was the next focus in our transformation.

We Needed A Key Supervisor

When we went through the exercise of what we wanted our lives to look like in five years a realization jumped out for both of us. We both loved the education aspect of what it was that we were doing. We liked helping others succeed. Steve had been much more involved through his consulting, coaching and speaking. I got a taste of it here and there through the training of my team, and through some training engagements we took on. (Can you see the beginnings of Kninja coming through?)

Frankly, I was tired and bored with my role at AIS Solutions. I no longer wanted to be the "go to" person on my team for client challenges and complex questions or projects. I wanted to focus on the growth of my business and my team and relinquish that role of being the one with all of the answers. (I know! Aren't you so proud! You probably thought you'd never hear those words from me.)

Also included in that two and five-year life plan, there was a lot of travelling. I mean, a lot of travelling. Travelling and speaking and educating. The only way that could ever happen was if I wasn't needed in the office on a day-to-day basis. I knew that this step was going to be a tough one on many levels. I needed a key supervisor on my team.

I actually had been trying to find this key person for several years already, and had been unsuccessful. My first attempt crashed and burned because I had put my faith in the wrong person. I had invested 11 months into the relationship teaching them all I knew, how I thought, what I said, why I said it, only to have them leave, start their own firm and take clients with them. (Not that I'm bitter or anything….I've just had to rely on my belief in karma.)

> **STEVE'S SLANT**
> Putting your hope into a new team member and working closely with them while sharing your knowledge is critical to the success of any business. But, on the rare occasion that the knowledge sharing, time and energy you invest in them blows up in your face and they quit…it can be traumatic and painful.
> This is when you must remind yourself of the abundance mindset. There is no alternate right path.
> Don't ask yourself "What if I train them - share my knowledge with them and they leave?" The far more important question to ask is "What if you don't train them and they stay?" How will that work out for the growth and success of your firm?
> When it happens, take some time to be "ticked off." Then move on and find someone else to train. Sometimes I have to remind Juliet of this more than once.

What that first attempt taught me was that I had to pay more attention to the ethics of the person in this role. Our second attempt had us promote from within, but we found that there wasn't enough higher level accounting knowledge to succeed in the role, as the team started bypassing them and came to me. The third attempt we went the extreme opposite and hired a CA with lots of high level knowledge. But they didn't understand the nuances of the accounting software from the bookkeeping perspective and so the team started bypassing them again and coming to me.

Do you see a pattern here? I did. And I was determined with all of those attempts that I was only honing in on what the skillset needed to look like in that role, and that I would then find that person. I knew that they were out there, I just hadn't found them yet, but I would.

"As an entrepreneur you must learn to embrace failure. You will try many things that don't work, until they do. Failures are part of the journey, but quitting is not." - Stephen Loates

---

I've already told you about some of my horror stories with trying to fill this key supervisor position. It's probably the toughest role to fill in a growing practice for a couple of reasons:

1. **You are looking for you.** Right? Aren't you though? Up until now, this role has been filled by you. So when you are trying to find someone to do the things that you've been doing, naturally, you start looking for someone who thinks like you, acts like you, and more importantly, will do the job like you. Well, stop. Just stop. You aren't going to find you. And you actually don't want you. You are an entrepreneur and likely can accomplish a lot of different things. You won't excel at all of them, but on some you will. This function might even be one of those...or it might not. But it doesn't matter because when filling this role, you want someone who is going to excel in it. So don't make the mistake of putting tasks and responsibilities on this position that require completely different skillsets. We've made that mistake and it was not a success for either us or our team. Once you've identified what the skillset is that you need for this person, find the person who excels in *that* skillset.

2. **They have to serve two masters.** What does that mean? This Right Hand, Account Manager, Account Supervisor, Team Leader, whatever you want to call this position - this is probably one of the most difficult roles in the organization because they really have two different people that they need to keep happy - and these two sets of people may

sometimes have conflicting expectations.

a) *Yourself* - Obviously they report to you. They need to take things off your plate and do them well

b) *Your Team* - As a team leader, they also have to meet the needs of your team. They have to motivate them, manage them, discipline them, and be their boss, their friend, their confidante.

Yeah, but you used to do all that, and then some. So what's the big deal with someone else having to do it? (See, I'm in your head, that's what you were thinking wasn't it?)

Easy. You're the boss. Not only did you not have someone else to report to or looking over your shoulder (and don't do this, by the way), you team couldn't go over your head, or around you, to someone else because you were it. This key supervisor isn't. The team knows it, and they can and will go over his or her head and come to you if they don't like the answer they've already received.

So do yourself a big favour - if the person in your team leader role is the right person - **DON'T** undermine them with the rest of your team.

> "Management is doing things right; leadership is doing the right things." - Peter Drucker

So we've told you that you need this role, well, how do you figure out what to get them to do? Where to get them started? Are we just going to end the chapter here? And have you fend for yourself? We may not have the answer, but let me share with you how I came up with what was delegated to this role.

I'm a control freak. Did I mention that? I think I did. So letting go of anything that was in my domain was tough for me. I had way too much on my plate. I knew that. I actually didn't even want to be doing some of the things that I was doing. I also knew that. But when it came to actually letting go of anything, it was SOOOO hard for me. I was part of an Executive Mastermind group at the time, and this was a suggestion that one of the other group members gave to me, someone who was running a $20 million dollar company, with numerous direct reports, and it worked really well.

As you are working, make a list of what tasks you are performing. Be specific. Don't just say something like "Client Work". List out "Processing Accounts Payable for Client X," "Reviewing Tax Return for Client Y." Now, next to the task you've listed, think about how much you enjoy doing it and then give it a rating of 1 - 10. Do this for every task that you are doing for two or three weeks. (Longer if your tasks vary a lot throughout the month.) Whether it's advertising, marketing, meetings, sales, client work, everything. And the rating is fundamental. Don't just list the tasks, but make sure that you are rating them as well.

A couple of things will come out of the exercise.

1. You'll see how much you actually do. You'll feel like a rock star. Look at me and how productive I am and how much responsibility I have. I am awesome! You are. But now let go of that mentality. What you want to do is leverage your time, not do everything.

2. You'll see a pattern of the things that you are enjoying doing, and the things that you aren't. There is absolutely no right or wrong answer to what should appear in your 10 ratings. It's your business, and you are unique, so your tens are your tens.

Once you've compiled this list, look at the commonalities of the items which received a rating below five. Those are the tasks you are going to delegate. Identify what skillset is needed in a person that will need to do those tasks. That's who you hire.

As I said, it doesn't matter what those tasks are. Yours are going to be completely different from mine. And that's okay. Your business is different than mine. You are different than me. That's the great thing about being a business owner - you get to decide what you want to do!

So you are probably thinking to yourself, "Well, that doesn't sound right!" That is way too self-serving! Why should I only delegate the things that I don't like to do; shouldn't I give them some stuff that's fun too? Have you ever read, or maybe even said, something like the following on a bookkeeping website, brochure or networking event? "You didn't go into business to do bookkeeping, but we did, so let us do it for you?" Or "Let us do your bookkeeping so that you can do what you love and the reason you opened your business."

I'm sure that you have; it's a pretty common theme for marketing bookkeeping services. Well, why do you have a different set of rules for yourself? Why are you doing things in your business that you don't love to do? And just because you don't love them doesn't mean that there isn't someone who will love them. The key is to find that person.

If we take it back to the bookkeeping example, most business owners don't like bookkeeping, but we do and we actually went into business so that we could do more of it!

One last thing. Don't judge yourself on what it is that you like or don't like to do. Don't think that you "should" keep this part of the job because it's the right thing to do. Keep what you love. Life is too short to do it any other way.

"If you don't love what you do, you won't do it with much conviction or passion." - Mia Hamm

---

We Needed Stronger Systems And Processes

Let's recap a bit, as the last couple of chapters have all been revolving around the same topic and I want to ensure that we remember what we are talking about!

In late 2015, we amended our mission and vision to be recognized as the standard against which all other bookkeepers and bookkeeping firms are measured. That was our lofty goal, and we knew that we needed to make some changes internally to accomplish this.

#1 - We were doing too many things

#2 - We needed a key supervisor

Those have both been covered in the last two sections,

so now we are onto the last thing that we identified as needing to change:

#3 - We needed stronger systems and processes

This last focus shift went hand in hand with both of the first two changes we needed to implement. By narrowing our focus on the services we were going to provide, the tools to provide them, and who we wanted to provide them to, we could then create more detailed processes that could be replicated across clients and team members.

I also knew that for the supervisor role to be successful this time, and for me to take a step back, I needed the ability to document what it was that I did so that someone else could do it.

I'm not going to tell you that it was easy. Any of it. Not the first, second or third step. But in order to move our business to the next phase in our evolution we had no choice. This was late 2015.

This first step seemed fairly easy in theory, a little more challenging in practice. Steve and I sat down on a beach, with our customary mudslides* in hand ---this has always been how we did our best brainstorming -- and identified our ideal client persona.

(*Mudslide recipe - since this drink was a pretty fundamental part of our evolution we thought you might like the recipe - we

certainly didn't invent it, but in some small way it may have helped invent us. :-) It is a mix of vodka, Kahlua and Bailey's Irish Cream. It is awesome and must be served very, very cold. Blender required.)

Here's how we did it:

#1 - Review our existing book of clients and rate them 1 to 10.

"10" - We loved working with them.

"1" - We let their calls go to voicemail, or had this awful feeling in the pit of our stomachs when we saw their name on the call display.

We wanted more "10" clients, so tried to identify what they had in common. Was it industry? Size? Mindset? Processes?

We made a list of questions that could be asked in the sales process to help identify them.

Then we went through the same exercise with those clients that garnered a "1" rating. We didn't want any more of those clients so we needed to identify similarities with those clients as well as questions that could be asked to help us determine they would be 1's before we took them on as clients.

#2 - Once we had this list, we started changing the messaging on our website to attract this new ideal client. The language, the imagery -- it was all to attract these "10" clients. We also created a questionnaire that prospective clients had to fill out <u>before</u> our discovery call. Although this reduced the number of inquiries we received, it significantly improved our closing ratio on those inquiries. We found that those business owners willing to fill in the questionnaire were generally qualified leads for us.

#3 - We also started to examine the metrics around the engagement with all of our clients.

1. What was their monthly fee?
2. How much time did we spend on them?
3. Were they profitable?
4. Were they on the platform we were using going forward?

We then divided our entire client base into three categories:

Green - Those who we loved working with, fit our ideal client persona, were profitable for us and were exactly the type of client that we could grow with together.

Yellow - Those clients who met three of the four criteria above and had the potential to become a green client with just a little tweaking

Red - The last category was made of clients who only met one or none of the criteria. They were either going to be impossible to convert to green clients, or we had been subsidizing their bookkeeping for so long that making them profitable would have been a shock to the monthly fee. Interestingly enough, most of our clients with a one or two rating fell into this category also.

We began implementing change with the red clients. So here's the thing. I saw the numbers. I sliced and diced those metrics, but the thought of letting them go if we couldn't turn them around was so painful. Many of them had been with us for a number of years.

Here's a perfect example - we had one client who we were billing $795 a month. At the end of our analysis, we realized that we made about $18 a month profit on them. That's not a typo - less than $20 a month, only $216 a year. And, they were taking up significant bandwidth for the team in terms of both time and frustration. You would think that it would be a no brainer for me to let them go. I could fill all of that time with more ideal clients, that we would enjoy working with, that we could help more effectively and have more fun! Yet I couldn't. I still could taste the fear of not knowing how we were going to make payroll, or would we have to cash in more RRSP's (that's a Canadian Retirement Savings Plan), or dip into our savings, that I couldn't get myself to give away revenue, even if it was sucking the life out of our business.

What does that say about me? That I'm human. And I'm not perfect. And it's why you need more than one person to help you with this exercise. Because sometimes we need someone objective to remind us of our value and our worth, and that the world will fill that void that you create.

I know. It makes no logical sense, and I'm a pretty logical person…..most of the time.

So, with Steve silently whispering in my ear that this was the right step (remember, this is operations, so falls under my domain), we started removing "red" clients where we couldn't move them to yellow or green status.

> **STEVE'S SLANT**
> I do remember some very heated debates around this time but I certainly don't remember "silently whispering" in Juliet's ear. Not really my style.
> Seriously, we both knew it needed doing, but it is

> never easy when you are dealing with emotions and people. We had relationships with a number of our "red" clients - we liked many of them, but if we were going to move forward this needed doing.

I'd love to tell you that we got rid of all of our red clients, moved all of our yellow up to green status, and did it quickly and easily because we rock. But this isn't a fairy tale, or a fiction book, and I don't want to tell you things just to make us sound like we've got it all under control. What I want is to have you feel, and truly believe, that you're not alone in feeling this way. That others are going through the same challenges and it's not as easy as it appears on social media or in some presentation at a conference. In fact, it's damn hard most days.

So back to our transformation.

"What the caterpillar calls the end, the rest of the world calls a butterfly." - Lao Tzu

We did let go of some red clients, like the $18 a month profit client, because he wasn't willing to work with us, and thought that we were charging him too much money already. We moved a couple into yellow status.

But we still kept a bunch of reds. I couldn't let them go until much later when we had replaced the income of the red clients I'd already released. So if you struggle with letting go of clients like I did, that's what I would recommend. Let go of one, replace that income with the right client, then let go of the next red. Sure, it's a slower process to get the right clients, and you won't experience any revenue growth for a time period, but it may help you sleep at night, or continue paying your bills.

And to those of you who are brave souls and can just cut those limbs off in one fell swoop….I so envy you.

The other thing that we did to scale back on doing too many things was narrow our tech stack. We already told you that we eliminated accounting packages and only started focusing on QBO, but we also narrowed down the third party programs that we supported alongside the accounting platform.

Let me give you an example - payroll. This was a service we offered to our clients and wanted to continue offering it. But, we were processing payroll for our clients with probably five or six different payroll platforms. We scaled this back to two (one is ideal, but all of our clients didn't fit with just the one option.)

Wagepoint was our "go to". Only if our client's

payroll was too complex for the functionality of Wagepoint was this second option considered. And it was us who made this determination, not the client. And it was the anomaly. I think that we only had two clients in total whose payroll couldn't be managed with the functionality of Wagepoint, and they were our largest clients.

Here is what this allowed us to do. Streamline and systematize. Using six different payroll providers meant that my team had to know six different programs. No big deal, since they already were working with them, and knew them, Right?

Wrong. When the mid-month payroll dates rolled around and it was a payroll day, it meant that they had to switch between these six programs, usually before noon, to complete payroll submissions.

You can see where I'm going with this, can't you?

Imagine the thought processes that they had to go through:

1. Which client am I working on?

2. What are the anomalies I need to know about this client's payroll? (Check their Teamwork project task list.)

3. What software do I use for their payroll?

4. What's that login password?

5. Switch gears from processing payroll in the previous program.

6. Remember to sync/export/manually enter the payroll numbers in QBO.

7. Rinse and repeat with the next client.

That's a lot of steps. But more importantly, #5 required a lot of brain power.

Now look at my streamlined workflow:

#1 and #2 are the same.

1. Which client am I working on?

2. What are the anomalies I need to know about this client's payroll? (Check their Teamwork project.)

3. Process in Wagepoint (Already logged in from working on the previous client)

4. **No longer needed**

5. **No longer needed**

6. Sync with QBO

You'll see that not only did this new process remove two steps, it also simplified the steps that remained and prevented my team from having to switch mental gears with every payroll being run, and that is what was vital.

It may not seem like a big deal, but in fact, it's a bigger deal than removing the two steps. Changing mental gears not only takes time, which is money, but it's also where the mistakes happen.

I think that we've already mentioned that our goal is to shave seconds off tasks, which add up to minutes and hours for our firm. Multiply that time saving for one person, by 10 people in our firm at that time, 14 people now, and you can see where I'm going with this. Just by scaling back to one product for payroll, we did save hours. The service to our client was the same - their employees got paid - and I would even argue that it got better because there were less mistakes and work flowed smoother.

Now duplicate that decision across the other services that you provide. Even sticking with payroll, what if you standardized the process so that all of your clients submitted their hours or timesheets to you in the same way. Would that not save you some brain power as well?

What else could you do that would impact your

practice? That could impact your bandwidth and efficiencies? And, most importantly increase your effectiveness for your client?

LESSONS LEARNED:

1. Consistent delivery of services and scalability can only happen when you have the right systems and the right people.
2. Stop trying to be all things to all people. Specialize as much as you possibly can.

7 BROWN BELT
– LET'S START A NEW BUSINESS (2016)

Brown Belt: A brown belt is maturing and beginning to realize the fruits of their hard work.

We are now in the spring of 2016. We had scaled back on services/apps/clients and had hired an accounting supervisor in February of 2016. I must admit, I was beside myself and so happy that I had someone in place to take away the things that I no longer wanted to do for AIS Solutions.

In late 2015/early 2016, Steve and I also made the decision to start Kninja - a new business venture we will talk about later on. We had been talking about it for probably the last few years, and quite honestly were hoping that someone else would build something so that we didn't have to, but there was no indication that was going to become a reality. So we made the decision to build it ourselves. That meant also, that this supervisor role was going to be even more critical, because it would allow me to focus my time on building Kninja, which I realized is also where my passion lay.

Steve and I may take a while to make a decision, but once we do, we jump in with both feet, and creating Kninja was no exception. We decided that we were going to launch Kninja in Toronto in December at the Canadian QuickBooks Connect Conference. (More details on what Kninja is and why we started it in the coming chapters.)

In order for that timeline to happen I needed to ensure that everything I was doing for AIS was being done by Andrea and being done well. So I went into system overdrive.

In 2015, scaling back our services and our tech stack made our business easier to systematize. Less exceptions, so basically also less processes. My goal was to be able to dedicate the majority of my time on Kninja by June 2016, which meant that I needed Andrea up and running at full speed in four months. I know, pretty ambitious, but you probably see this as a pattern for us. We pretty much have lived by this quote "Most people tend to overestimate what they can do in a day, and underestimate what they can do in a year."

I was excited about starting work on Kninja; my brain was working on it all the time, even when I wasn't supposed to be working on it and focusing on AIS Systems. It was also the first time, in a long time, that I was excited about going to work, because I saw my ability to do something else, something that I was passionate about. But first....I just needed to get Andrea up and running. And that's exactly what I did. I spent a lot of hours with Andrea doing massive brain dumps of what I was doing, how I was doing them, and why I did them. She was eager to learn, so it seemed like it was a great combination.

Yes, I created a bunch of systems, but for a lot of things I did the brain dump and then relied on her to document and implement. We had meetings twice a week at the beginning, and then moved to once a week as she was moving forward. I was feeling really good about everything, and our project management tool, Teamwork, had never had so many documented processes for our firm.

We were good to go in June 2016, and I pulled back from AIS Solutions and poured my focus and energy into Kninja.

The Birth Of Kninja

So what is Kninja and what does the name mean? We get asked that question all the time. So here's the 30 second elevator pitch on Kninja. *Kninja is an online educational and support community for bookkeepers and accounting professionals, by bookkeepers. Our industry is undergoing such a massive disruption that it is tough to keep up and learn everything that has to be learned. That is why we created Kninja. To help other bookkeepers grow their firm and stay ahead of the cloud technology curve.*

Yes, that's a mouthful, but here is how it started.

I've already mentioned that Steve and I do our best brainstorming and come up with our most ingenious ideas while we are sitting on a beach with mudslides in our hands and our ears tuned to the sound of the ocean. It's probably because we have no distractions. No day-to-day stuff is floating through our minds, and we have the opportunity to just let our minds wander. Sometimes the ideas turn out to be really bad, but most of the time they tend to move our business and our life forward. Although, if you listen to the experts, even bad ideas are good, because you've identified what doesn't work so you can find something that does.

Kninja was no exception, although it wasn't called Kninja then. We had probably been talking about it since QBConnect 2014, when we were trying to figure out how to get our team up to speed with QBO as quickly as possible. We knew that the bookkeeping industry was changing rapidly with no signs of a slowdown. If anything, all indications were that the pace of change was only going to increase. It was going to get harder and harder to stay current with all of the current changes and look after providing the best service for our clients.

As our own team grew internally, we also felt that we were continuously reinventing the wheel and starting proper cloud bookkeeping training from the beginning. There was no leveraging happening. Every time we hired someone new, we had to dedicate a person on our team or have multiple people train this new team member. Most of the people joining us had no experience with QBO and so we had to invest the time to get them up to speed.

In 2015, we also launched an apprenticeship program in our office and found that we were struggling to find them a resource that they could follow step by step to get them up to speed quickly.

We found that we were jumping from one website to YouTube to Facebook groups, to Intuit training, and there was no clear path for us to follow, nor any consistency in what or how we were learning. Lots of good material….lots of people with their hearts in the right place….but no cohesion or organization.

And don't get me started on the apps and the ecosystems, and which apps work best for which industries, and how did we get our team to put it all together?

So Kninja started in our heads as something we needed to build internally. We honestly kept waiting, and hoping for someone else to build something that we could buy, but didn't see that coming on the horizon anywhere.

So Steve and I were sitting on this beach in late 2015 at one of our favourite resorts in the Mayan Riviera. Steve was patiently listening to me lament about how we couldn't get our new team up to speed fast enough, and how our current team had no bandwidth to train the new members the way that they needed to be trained. We needed to create some kind of training system that they went through to alleviate the burden on myself and our existing team.

I was thinking internally only, worried about my little kingdom. Steve is the big thinker and said that if we are struggling so much, isn't everyone? Let's create it and then sell it to others who are also struggling. In the words of our coach - let's leverage it.

And that is how the idea was born. We spent the rest of the afternoon and the remainder of our beach days mapping out what it could look like. And why would we stop just at the training side? Bookkeepers struggle with sales and marketing and managing their practice or their staff, so why wouldn't we make it a platform where we could share all of the mistakes that we made, as well as all of our learnings?

As you can see, we don't ever seem to think small.

The Kninja Name

We've told you what Kninja is, but where did we get the name? Honestly, this isn't going to be of much value to learn this story, or maybe it will, but it's certainly a question we are asked all the time, so here goes.

We had a lot of name options going through our heads when we were getting set to market. If you were to ask me if I remember any of those other names, I don't. I just know that they weren't as cool. Most of the names centered around "Ninja, "as that is what I've been calling my team for years, and our team name is always The Number Ninjas, when we enter anything. But we wanted the name and the website URL to be short, so www.thenumberninjas.com was way too long. And it didn't accurately represent the program, because it was going to be about so much more than only the numbers of your business. The URL www.ninja.com was not available, so we tried to come up with something close. Ninja Bookkeeper also seemed to be more common as others in the industry were starting to use it as well, and we needed it to be different and memorable. I've always felt that the name AIS Solutions wasn't really creative but the thought of rebranding from scratch when we have some name recognition makes no sense, so I didn't want to make the same mistake here. So we started to Google other Japanese names, and synonyms to ninja. Nothing really exciting or catchy. Then we thought about Ninja Knights, which then evolved to Kninja, pronounced (nɪndʒə) according to Wikipedia (but I don't even know how to pronounce that!). Basically it's pronounced the same as Ninja, with a silent K.

The amazing thing was when I looked it up online, I found that it's actually a word in an urban slang dictionary.

Here's the definition:

Noun: 1. The top elite ninjas of any ninja clan, "ninja knights" if you will.
2. Ninjas so sneaky, even the 'k" in their name is silent.

I don't love the second part of that definition, because sneaky and bookkeeping really aren't two words that should be uttered in the same sentence, but the first definition was exactly what we wanted to represent.

Seeing that definition also inspired our tag line - *"Don't just be a ninja bookkeeper...become a Kninja bookkeeper."*

I must admit that I loved the name, but had a hard time selling it to Steve. Remember that marketing falls under Steve's domain, so ultimately the end decision on name and branding fell to him. But I pushed hard. Really hard. And after a lot of coercion with several fine California Merlots, he relented. And so the name was born, and the branding soon followed.

Again, we needed it to be different, so wanted a Kninja mascot to be representing us out in social media, and we had a Kname the Kninja contest. Sometimes we may have gone too far with the K's, but really...it's fun. We have become known as the Kninja Knetwork with our Kninja Knowledge Webinars. And of course the names had to follow the same theme, so Knina was born.

I could write an entire book just about Knina and the mascot, trying to get a 3D printed mascot and the hoops I jumped through only to find that it couldn't be made in anything other than porcelain, which made no sense for an adventurous Kninja on the conference circuit. I could see myself dropping her so easily as she scaled signs and rocks and hurdles in the industry.

The branding side of Kninja was fun for me, and we had a LOT of fun with Knina as our mascot.

But the real fun was in creating the content for the platform.

I didn't realize how much I would enjoy it, until I started doing it.

After much discussion, we ended up determining that the platform would contain three tracks –

LEARN was my baby, BUILD was Steve's and then we worked collaboratively on the MANAGE Track.

It was exciting. I was doing something new. I knew that what I was doing was going to be leveraged internally by my team and training, but also that the possibilities were endless as to how many more people we could help.

Sure, it was frustrating at times. Because in typical Steve and Juliet fashion, we bit off a lot, and gave ourselves a really tight time frame. Our target was to launch at the QBConnect Conference in Toronto which was December 2016, and in the six month time frame we gave ourselves (thinking that was so much time), we had to build a new website, market the website, find an educational platform, learn the platform, build the content on that platform and somewhere in there have a life. Needless to say, I'm not sure we had much of a life, and I learned so much more than I probably wanted to about video editing.

But we hit our target and launched the first week of December 2016. I must admit I was beside myself when we signed up our first Kninja client at QBConnect.

As an aside, as we were building out our Kninja platform, in September, we were also awarded the title of Bookkeeping Firm of the Year by the Institute of Professional Bookkeepers of Canada (IPBC). We were so busy with building Kninja that I didn't even attend the conference that year, so needless to say was quite stunned when we made the finalist list, and then woke up the morning after the conference with my phone and social media accounts exploding with congratulations. It was awesome. And both Steve and I were so proud of our team.

So back to Kninja. Actually, it's back to AIS. The month of December 2016 was a whirlwind as we launched, signed up new members, marketed, and worked out some kinks in the logistics of our platform, because nothing ever works out exactly the way that you think it will.

Enter January 2017. I took a deep breath, and then looked at how AIS was faring. I really looked at AIS, and our clients and our team, which I hadn't done for almost six months. So here's where things went sideways. Because you knew I was leading up to things not running smoothly, right?

I realized that there were holes in those awesome systems I had created. I hadn't covered all the contingencies I thought that I had. I hadn't thought of everything! You may not be surprised, but I was. I was so sure that my systems and processes were rock solid. But they weren't. Not by a long shot. Quite honestly, I was really upset. Because I was so sure.

But Steve wasn't surprised, and retained his positive outlook on everything as he tends to do. "That's awesome he said!" (I know, right?) "It's awesome, because now you know what we have to do to fix it, and just think as to how much stronger it is all going to be when we're done. You pretty much walked away from the business for six months. And it's still there. It's still running. You still have a team. You still have a business. You are closer now than you've ever been to achieving that definition of a business." Remember it from earlier in the book - "A commercial profitable enterprise that *runs without you*".

> **"You don't learn to walk by following rules. You learn by doing, and by falling over and then getting back up again." - Richard Branson**

I hate it when he's right. But he was. So my head went down again and for the next month I worked on improving what I thought were those rock solid systems. I added more steps into my Teamwork projects for each task. I filled in the gaps for things that were in my head and nowhere else. Because we now knew what those gaps were.

LESSONS LEARNED:

1. All of the hard work that you put into your systems will pay off. But they won't be perfect the first time.
2. So don't be like me, and expect them to be. They will be constantly evolving, so accept it.
3. Accept that the first time there will be gaps, but that you can fill them.

8 RED BELT
– THE FINAL CHAPTER – FOR NOW (2017)

The spring of 2017 was pretty uneventful for us in terms of change. We were maintaining the status quo on our services, and our client base, and our team. Instead of changing things, we were shoring up our foundation - adding to our systems and processes, growing surely and steadily. If I wasn't working on systems and processes for AIS Solutions, I was working on content for Kninja, we were conducting Kninja Knowledge Webinars with industry leaders, or we were involved with one of our Kninja Mentoring groups.

The mentoring groups were quite honestly awesome. I was surprised at how much I was enjoying it and how rewarding it was. I was doing one on one mentoring with individuals new to the cloud for Intuit Canada, but Steve and I were also providing group mentoring through Kninja. There were typically five people in a group and we met virtually once a week. We tried to organize the groups so that everyone in the group was at a similar level in their business, so that the challenges people were facing were alike.

The weekly meetings were something I looked forward to, because I could tangibly see how we were able to help people. Sure, Kninja was growing and I "knew" that we were helping the members through the content we were creating. But I didn't "see" it. I wasn't interacting with them. With our group mentoring, it was so different. I saw the changes that were taking place in their businesses. I saw what helping them identify their 90-day goals and their vision for the future could do for them, as it had done with us.

Let's talk a little bit about planning and goal setting. We were still following the methodology of Goal Setting and 90 day plans every quarter since 2011 - over 25 quarterly plans and goals to this point. And if you don't believe that it works, let me tell you that it does. Here's two perfect examples.

In the year of 2014 we had set an annual revenue

target for ourselves. It was big. And scary. But realistic, if we worked hard. And the goal for hitting this target was new light fixtures for our front entranceway at home that I had been eyeing forever. We were still struggling financially in 2014, and so frivolous upgrades weren't really in our budget back then. We hit the target. We bought the light fixtures. And as much as I love the fixtures on their own, every time I look at them, I am reminded of the sensation of hitting that goal.

> **STEVE'S SLANT**
> Goal setting is mandatory to keep you focused and motivated. If you don't know where you are trying to go how will you know when you get there? All too often I run into other business owners who don't have a plan. They know they want to something more, something different, but they haven't taken the time to sit down and map it out. To make a plan as to how they are going to get there.
> I am always reminded of something our coach said to us on many occasions, "if you want something you've never had, you must be willing to do something you've never done."
> If you want to achieve something different for your own life - make a plan - map it out - visualize it. The more clearly you can see it, the better chance you have of achieving it. And for goodness sake don't forget the most important part of goal setting - the part we often forget - reward yourself when you achieve the goal. The reward doesn't need to be huge (although you will

> see from below that Juliet didn't follow that path). When we started out on this process, sometimes the reward we would set would be something as simple as giving ourselves permission to take the day off and do something we loved but never made time for. Don't think that it needs to be a material reward at all; just make sure you reward yourself with something that is important to you.
>
> Another great quote that I often hear ringing in my head when we talk about goal setting is Jim Rohn's words: "It is not the goal that is important - it is what it makes of you in working to achieve that goal." Wise words. Thank you again, Mr. Rohn.

Fast forward to 2017, and the rewards for my goals were getting loftier, and more expensive. In the spring of 2017, my car lease was up for renewal and I was due for a new vehicle. I set a goal for myself that in order to get the car that I really wanted, I had to get enough new Kninja subscriptions over the coming quarter to cover the difference between my existing car payment and the payment of the car I really wanted. I was motivated. I created this countdown sheet which was plastered everywhere. I needed 81 new members to get the car of my dreams.

```
81 80 79 78 77 76 75 74 73 72 71 70 69 68
67 66 65 64 63 62 61 60 59 58 57 56 55
54 53 52 51 50 49 48 47 46 45 44 43 42
41 40 39 38 37 36 35 34 33 32 31 30 29 28
27 26 25 24 23 22 21 20 19 18 17 16 15 14 13
12 11 10 9 8 7 6 5 4 3 2 1
```

Every time we got a new member, I would cross off a number.

The desktop pictures on my laptop would rotate between this countdown, pictures of the car, pictures of the car with my license plate on it (the joy of Photoshop), and motivational sayings telling me how awesome I was.

Here was the end result of all that goal setting and crazy motivation:

We did try something completely different in the spring of 2017 with our team community outreach. As you saw earlier, we tried to pick an annual charity to support even though our 24 Hour Relay for Hope left us exhausted. We ranged from a Coldest Night of the Year walk in support of the Homeless, to closing the office for a day in December and helping out at a charity with a Christmas drive. As we are wont to do, in 2017 we aimed a little higher and thought that we would set up our own charitable event. We partnered with The Compassion Society of Burlington and organized our very first Steps to Success event. It was a three day event to help women who were either entering the workforce for the first time, or re-entering the workforce. It was an event designed to help them feel confident and ready to tackle that job interview. We had volunteers to review their resume and prep them for job interviews, stylists to help them choose an interview outfit, complete with shoes and accessories, and then hair and makeup stylists to give them a fresh new look.

The next couple of pages have the flyer and some photos from the event.

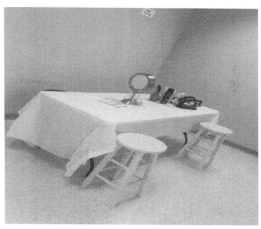

THE KNINJA WAY

It was amazing. The outpouring of donations that we received, and the transformation that we saw in the women that walked through that door made all of it worthwhile. And it planted the seed for an AIS Foundation.

But I digress…completely. The year 2017 was running pretty smoothly for us. Steve and I were happy with how everything was growing at AIS Solutions, and we were both enjoying working on our new baby - Kninja. I'll admit it, we got a little complacent. And comfortable. Again.

Application, What Application? (July 2017)

It was July 2017 and a lovely summer evening. Steve and I were sitting outside on our back deck, drinking some wine (what else?) and talking about the future. Here's a snippet of our conversation on that evening:

Steve: Did you ever get that application in for that Intuit contest?

Me: No, I haven't. There's no way that we could win that, so I didn't.

Steve: But you had a picture taken with the team for it, and told them that we were going to enter it?

Me: I know. I started to. I looked at the application

and it was asking us for reasons why we were so different, and I was having a lot of trouble figuring out what to write, so I stopped.

Steve: I can have a look at it. When's the deadline?

Me: I don't know. Let me check. (Pull out my iPad). Midnight tonight.

Steve: Ok, let's work on it now and just put it in. You never know what might happen.

And so we did. We got our application in at about 11:35 that night, a half hour before the midnight deadline of "that Intuit contest".

Here's our picture submission.

For those of you that don't know, Intuit holds an incredible contest every year called The Firm of the Future. It's a Global contest, and involved almost 1,000 firms from Australia, Canada, United Kingdom and the United States. The premise is to choose companies who represent the future of the industry by exemplifying characteristics of "Firms of the Future. The first stage was submitting a written application answering some of their questions, as well as a picture illustrating you as a Firm of the Future. A panel of judges at the Intuit US offices chooses a country representative from each of the four countries, who then compete for a Global Title. This is the "Intuit contest" that Steve was referring to and which we put in our application at the eleventh hour.

The Big Apple

Life moved along that summer. I was turning 50 that August and was given this amazing surprise birthday gift by Steve of a trip to New York City. I had no idea where we were going until we were on the way to the Buffalo airport the morning of our flight. (The ladies reading this are probably thinking, how in the world did you know what to pack? Thankfully, my daughter made sure that I had the appropriate shoes and clothes.) Steve and I implemented a "totally disconnected" policy a few years ago. When we go away on vacation, we are disconnected from the office. No phone calls from the team. No emails being checked. Out of office message on, which says that there is no access to email. This week in New York was no different.

While we were creating these amazing family memories, totally disconnected from the world back home, we received the following email on August 26, 2017.

> **HelloWorld**
> fulfillment@eprizefulfillment.com
>
> We're happy to inform you that you are one of the four finalists in the 2017 Intuit Firm of the Future Contest! You've won a trip for two (2) members of the Firm to San Jose, California to attend 2017 QuickBooks Connect (November 15-17) and a $5,000 USD cash prize (or approximately 6,750CAD) fulfilled as check, which has an approximate value of $10,300 CAD. You are also in the running for the Grand Prize. Congratulations!
>
> To confirm your win, please complete a Declaration of Compliance, Liability & Publicity Release ("Declaration"). Please note at the bottom of the Declaration who the accountant will be that will be traveling on the trip. This accountant will be required to complete a Travel Companion Liability & Publicity Release.
>
> ==Please fully complete the Declaration and submit a signed original to HelloWorld, the administrator of this promotion. It must be received within 4 calendar days of this email.== If you do not return your Declaration within this timeframe, we will need to select another winner.
>
> The Sponsor requests that you keep your win as a finalist confidential until it is announced publicly on/or after September 12, 2017. This includes not sharing the news online via social media, on your company website or any other external form of communication until after the news is made public. The Sponsor appreciates your participation in keeping your status as runner finalists confidential and will be contacting you shortly to discuss the details of the next phase, which is the filming of your video for the world wide vote.

Read the highlighted box **carefully**. We weren't due home until the evening of August 30th. Which meant that there would be no email checking until the morning of August 31st. The only person that the email was sent to was me.

Do you see where I'm going with this story? On the 4th and last day that we had to accept this Canadian Finalist win, my phone starting ringing like crazy. First I got a call from someone I knew at Intuit Canada telling me to check my email. Within minutes, our team from the office called and texted myself and Steve for us to urgently call the office. The moderators of the contest had sent another email to me, received my out of office message and then called our office to get someone there to accept the declaration so we could be confirmed as the Canadian finalists.

Needless to say, we were stunned. Our team was beyond excited. Not only did we almost miss the deadline for entering the contest, we had a blip in our application and initially got disqualified, and then we almost missed the deadline for accepting, and this book would then have a completely different title, and ending. But we didn't. It must have been fate.

The months of September and October 2017 were a whirlwind. Preparing for the QBConnect conference in San Jose where they would make the Global Announcement for the winner, recording a video for the contest, writing a blog post on our Journey to the Firm of the Future, media interviews, preparing our social media blasts for the public voting portion of the contest, going dress shopping for what I was going to wear for the conference, and somewhere in there running two businesses. I don't think that I got much sleep in those two months, but I wouldn't trade it for anything.

Let me just jump back to the public voting section of the contest. Part of the contest and the choosing of the winner is based on public voting over a two-week period. We knew that we would have a *serious* disadvantage to the US contestant, just from the sheer differential in population between our countries. But we were determined. The incredible outpouring of support from our Canadian tribe was so amazing. Steve and I were beyond stunned at all of the people who put it in their reminders so that they could vote every day, and shared out on social media to garner more support for us. We were so humbled.

My parents were also beyond excited and rallying up all of their friends to vote for us as well. I had jokingly (or maybe not) told my mom that her role in all of this was to get the one billion people in India to vote for us. And she took her role very seriously. I still remember one of my cousins posting something on Facebook that they were celebrating something in their own lives. I don't recall what it was - a birthday, a wedding, some kind of really big announcement. My mom commented on their post, and I still remember it word for word today - "Congratulations! Great news! Did you remember to vote today? Like I said, she took her role very seriously.

Our dog, Godfrey (no, we didn't choose his name, he was a Rescue and arrived in our home with that name) along with Knina, became the faces of our social media campaign.

Here's a sample of two of our most popular posts:

We also did some Facebook live events, and tons of people across the industry brought us into their groups with live events to rally support. I still get goose bumps thinking about it all!

We also had this huge Canadian contingent down in San Jose supporting us! They all sat together for the big announcement, and we had shipped down Red and White pom-poms to give to them to share our Canadian pride.

I had so many people come up afterwards to tell us how they unfortunately sat behind the Canadians, and they certainly broke the mold of quiet, conservative Canadians.

We weren't able to take our entire team to be there with us unfortunately, but two members were with us. However, we did promise to conduct a Facebook "Live" for those who weren't able to make it, as well as for my parents and our daughter who stayed home from school that morning to watch.

If you are interested in watching the announcement, the video is on our [YouTube channel](https://www.youtube.com/watch?v=j5ZL31CQzCU&t=16s)

https://www.youtube.com/watch?v=j5ZL31CQzCU&t=16s

But what was most touching, and what we had no idea was going to happen, was that our team back home recorded *themselves* watching our Facebook Live and sent it to us so that they were a part of the excitement. That video is also on our [YouTube Channel.](https://www.youtube.com/watch?v=CVyz96yZgTw)

https://www.youtube.com/watch?v=CVyz96yZgTw

Needless to say, both Steve, myself and our team were all blown away when they announced us as the Global Winner for the Firm of the Future. It was not anything that we ever expected. We were called up to the big stage at QBConnect and sat with Rich Preece, Intuit's Global Accountant Segment Leader, where he interviewed us about our journey for about a half hour. Honestly, I don't remember it at all. And neither did Steve. When we left the Main Stage that day and finished the media interviews and photo shoot and accepted congratulations from all of the amazing people....when we finally made it back to our room before the Canadian dinner celebration, we both watched the Facebook "Live" we had recorded, because we couldn't even remember what we had said! So many people said that we looked so calm during our interview, and all I had been thinking was that my legs were shaking through the whole thing, and could everyone see them?

Here are some more of our social media posts when we won the big announcement in November:

Life when we returned home was more of the same excitement and positive energy, and we were all flying high for many months afterwards. Even Steve, who although very confident in all of our accomplishments, also still didn't really believe that we could win, because the title had never left the US since its inception. He was so sure that we weren't going to win, that he even agreed to having a cream pie thrown in his face by our team if we won! You can see how that turned out on our YouTube Channel: https://www.youtube.com/watch?v=pp7uAlV8VZw

It's now been almost a year since the Firm of the Future announcement in San Jose. So, what has the last year been like for us? We are asked that all the time. Quite honestly, it's been amazing. Not just from the honour of the recognition, but a couple of unexpected surprises arose from the entire experience.

#1 – The Community

I had always known that we were part of an incredible industry. Camaraderie and collaboration have always been something that we've been fortunate to experience, but this last year has been so far beyond anything we could imagine. I've been so lucky for many years to have a strong tribe of colleagues who have also become friends. But this last year, I've learned how strong and supportive this community is, from people that I had never previously met. The Canadian support that we saw was mind blowing leading up to the announcement, throughout the public voting process, but it was really afterwards that was astounding. I honestly thought that once the hoopla of the conference was over, the only one that would really to continue to care that we were the Global Firm of the Future would be myself and Steve and probably my mom and dad.

But that wasn't the case at all. People knew my name and introduced themselves online and at conferences and would share so much of their own personal journeys with me. They would share their similarities with my story, but tell me that they were inspired that they, too, could overcome the challenges because they saw that I had. Wow. It has all been such a humbling experience.

#2 – Team Pride

Both Steve and I were the ones front and centre for this experience and up on the various stage platforms. We've said throughout and at every opportunity, that we didn't get here alone, and that our incredible Kninja team were and continue to be, the key to the success that we've been able to achieve. What has surprised us is the amount of team pride that has come from this recognition and title. Our team has become more unified, more cohesive, more engaged in the success of other members on the team and the business overall. I cannot tell you how many times we have heard over the last 10 months "Of course we do, we're the Firm of the Future." If you missed the video which our team recorded of themselves watching the Firm of Future announcement last year – you can watch it on our YouTube Channel here

https://www.youtube.com/watch?v=CVyz96yZgTw

We had no idea they were going to do this, and we had told them we would broadcast it over Facebook Live because we weren't able to have them all in San Jose with us. This video says it better than we ever could.

As I mentioned earlier in the book, Steve had been

bugging me for about a year and a half that we needed to write a book, but I couldn't figure out why or what we could possibly offer. It wasn't until I had so many people I didn't know come up to us and tell us how we inspired them and how they had started out for the same reasons as me, that I knew that we finally needed to do this. Because what everyone sees is us up on that stage at the conference looking like we have it all together and that we are awesome, our team is awesome, our clients are awesome....you get the picture.

And I really wanted you to know that it's not perfect, never has been and I don't expect it ever will be. I wanted people who are feeling the same way that we did back in 2012 and 2013 to know that there is hope and there is a light at the end of the tunnel, and you can and will come out on the other side. That's the reason for this book, pure and simple.

LESSONS LEARNED:

1. Whenever you can, teach others. Nothing is more rewarding and as a side benefit you also learn how much you know and what else you need to learn.
2. Work hard. Have fun. Support your team, your clients and your community. And the rewards will follow.

THE KNINJA WAY

9 BLACK BELT
– ENJOY THE RIDE OR NEXT STEPS

Black Belt: The black belt seeks new, more profound knowledge and opportunities and begins to teach others helping them to grow and mature.

Wow. So we are done. For now. We've crammed eight years into these pages, and I know that some of the chapters went really fast. We focused on some years more than others - mostly the ones where we had the most challenges, but learned the most.

We do hope, though, that we've accomplished our goal within these pages. To let you know that you're not alone. To give you hope. To remind you that if we could do it, so could you!

Although this book is done, our story definitely isn't. As you've probably learned, Steve and I aren't ones for sitting still. I'm actually reminded of something that one of our tribe said to us at QBConnect Toronto a month after the Global Firm of the Future Award. We were talking about and trying to get feedback from those we trust and respect in the industry about how we could improve Kninja and ensure that it was covering relevant topics and pain points for the industry. And this gentleman said to us "Wow, now I know why you guys are Firm of the Future. You just won this Global Title and instead of sitting back and doing nothing but enjoying that, which most people would do, you guys are trying to figure out what you can do better."

And that, more than anything, is who we are. Always looking over the horizon.

So what's next? Well, Kninja 2.0 is around the corner,

getting ready for launch. We've listened to all the feedback we've received since it was originally launched and restructured the platform and type of content that we are creating to keep it more relevant, and we hope, more useful for those in our industry.

AIS Solutions hired its first full time, 100% virtual person, so I'm sure that there will be new things that we learn as we embark on this new model. Especially with our culture being so fundamental to who we are, ensuring that it thrives is so important to us.

As we usually do, we also are planning out into the future and looking to 2020. The goal for 2020 is to launch a Foundation for AIS. It's still in the preliminary stages, no name or branding yet, but its purpose is already clearly defined. "Our mission is to help women take that first or next step in business." To that end, we've made the decision that all proceeds from the sale of this book will be put aside as seed money to get this Foundation off the ground in 2020.

As much as I fought Steve initially on writing this book, I'm actually sad to see it come to an end. I feel like there is so much that I still want to share, and stories that I want to tell. But it's time. I know that. Time to send it off into the world. So I'll end off with our updated AIS Manifesto, which morphed from our Wall of Culture. The sign hangs proudly in the reception area of our office. I hope that if you are ever in our neck of the woods, you will drop by and visit us. We would love to meet you in person.

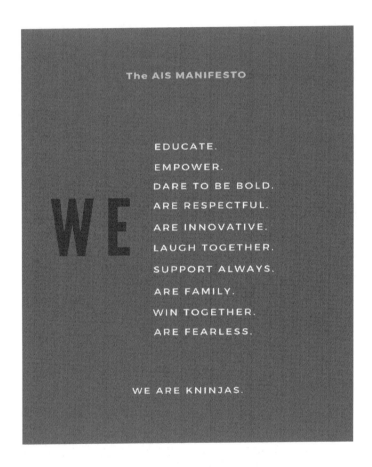

STAY IN TOUCH

Even though the book is done, don't be a stranger! We would still love to stay in touch with you.

Here's where you can find us:

Web:
www.aissolutions.ca
www.kninja.net

Facebook:
https://www.facebook.com/aissolutions/
https://www.facebook.com/kninjaknetwork

Twitter:
https://twitter.com/JulietAurora
https://twitter.com/SteveLoates
https://twitter.com/AISSolutions
https://twitter.com/kninjaknetwork

LinkedIn:
https://www.linkedin.com/in/julietaurora/
https://www.linkedin.com/in/steveloates/

Made in the USA
San Bernardino, CA
10 November 2019

59712274R00129